LEVERAGED BUYOUTS

A PRACTICAL INTRODUCTORY GUIDE TO LBOS

DAVID PILGER

HARRIMAN HOUSE LTD

3A Penns Road
Petersfield
Hampshire
GU32 2EW
GREAT BRITAIN

Tel: +44 (0)1730 233870
Email: enquiries@harriman-house.com
Website: www.harriman-house.com

First published in Great Britain and United States of America in 2012

ISBN: 978–0857–190–95–6

British Library Cataloguing in Publication Data
A CIP catalogue record for this book can be obtained from the British Library.

Set in Garamond and Gotham Narrow.

 Harriman House

This book is dedicated to Ashley. For your patience and support during the writing of this book – thank you.

CONTENTS

FIGURES

ABOUT THE AUTHOR

David Pilger is a founder and principal at Flex Banker LLC, a corporate advisory firm focused on providing corporate finance and capital raising advice to growing companies with innovative technologies. Flex Banker focuses on education, Ag-science, alternative energy, and manufacturing/industrial sectors as well as the financial sector. In addition to advising emerging growth companies with game-changing technology, he has been a consultant or advisor to large institutional clients such as Goldman Sachs, Morgan Stanley, and Pepsico to name a few.

David teaches corporate valuation and financial modeling and trains financial industry professionals at top financial institutions such as Paulson & Co., Barclays Capital, and other leading financial institutions at Blue Chip Career advisors.

Prior to working at Flex Banker, David specialised in senior bank debt at Goldman, Sachs & Co. He oversaw approximately $2 billion in the firm's bank loan structured trading and derivative portfolios. Before joining Goldman Sachs, he worked in investment banking at Merrill Lynch and Shinsei Bank in Tokyo, Japan, focusing on corporate advisory and M&A within the financial institutions sector.

David studied finance at the University of Virginia, earning a B.S. in Commerce. Upon graduating from the University of Virginia, he entered Princeton University, studying Japanese, and later went on to study advanced Japanese at Jouchi University in Tokyo, Japan.

Get the eBook of

LEVERAGED
BUYOUTS

for free

As a buyer of the printed version of this book you can download the electronic version free of charge.

To get hold of your copy of the eBook, simply point your smartphone camera at the code above (or go to **ebooks.harriman-house.com/leveragedbuyouts**).

PREFACE

WHAT THIS BOOK IS ABOUT

This book is designed to explain the logic, concepts and analytical techniques behind leveraged buyout analysis – in plain (and painless) English and with a practical emphasis.

It explains leveraged buyouts and everything involved in their analysis. It also contains a detailed step-by-step guide to the process of putting together an LBO analysis. This lays bare the analytical model most often used by practitioners in the investment industry, in a sequential narrative form. Readers should be able to take the techniques described in this book and create their own leveraged buyout analyses. A complete MS Excel version of the leverage buyout analysis can be found at **www.fin-models.com**.

WHO THIS BOOK IS FOR

This booked is designed for the individual who wants to learn the fundamental principles and modeling techniques of LBO analysis, as used by financial analysts in the investment banking industry.

With the modeling analysis approached from a practitioner's standpoint, it is assumed that the reader is most interested in a *practical* approach. The emphasis is on the approach a practitioner takes on a daily basis in preparing a leveraged buyout analysis. This is as opposed to an academic approach, which would be more focused on theory and leveraged buyouts as a concept (though the theory and concept is dealt with in the first few chapters).

WHAT KNOWLEDGE IS ASSUMED

It is assumed that the reader has had a previous introduction to financial statements (the income statement, balance sheet and cash flow statement) and rudimentary accounting concepts. A basic knowledge of what financial statements are as well as the function and purpose of the income statement, balance sheet and cash flow statement will be essential. However, the book does explain every element of an LBO analysis, which necessarily involves explaining aspects of financial statements as this analysis relates to them.

This book assumes that the reader will be using MS Excel as their spreadsheet software for creating an LBO analysis. It therefore also assumes that the reader has a very basic working knowledge of Excel. The formulaic functions within MS Excel are explained in detail, but it is taken for granted that the user has some basic understanding of MS Excel as a tool that can be used for financial analysis.

PART I
LEVERAGED BUYOUTS EXPLAINED

CHAPTER 1
WHAT IS AN LBO?

I f you're looking for a job or about to start a new job in investment banking or corporate finance you're probably going to have to know a thing or two about companies buying other companies. You may have picked up this book because you are just curious to know more about the workings of corporate finance and financial transactions. Well, you have come to the right place. But before we get started and dive into the makings of an LBO transaction, we first need to define what exactly an LBO is.

An LBO or leveraged buyout is, simply put, one company buying another company and using a large amount of debt to do it. That's it. So 'why all the fuss?' you might ask. Why does this type of transaction get set aside from other types of mergers and acquisitions? The answer lies in the inherent risks that go along with a transaction that is financed primarily with borrowed money.

There are a few things that we need to recognize about the debt that is used in a leveraged buyout transaction. The first is that the debt used to acquire the target company is often secured by the assets of the target. In other words, a potential buyer does not necessarily need to possess the financial means to purchase a target company. Instead, the target company just needs to have enough available collateral, in the form of its assets, to allow an outside buyer to obtain debt financing (secured by the target's assets) to pay for the cost of the transaction. Debt financing can also be secured by the assets of the buyer, but naturally using someone else's assets as collateral is always considered more attractive than pledging one's own assets as security for debt financing.

> An LBO is, simply put, one company buying another company and using a large amount of debt to do it.

The second point to mention about the debt is that it can come in the form of bonds or bank loans. In the case of bonds, this means that the debt is issued and typically sold to investors in the capital markets. There is a fixed coupon rate that the target company must pay to its creditors (i.e. the purchasers of the bonds), which is dictated under the terms of the bond at issuance. The high levels of debt associated with leveraged buyouts, relative to the amount of equity in the target company, often results in the bonds being rated as junk or below investment grade. As credit ratings are used to gauge the risk of default, it should come as no surprise that loading up a company with debt will naturally increase the risk of default – and the higher the risk, the higher the interest rate the market is going to demand for lending.

> Lending in an LBO is frequently syndicated amongst a group of banks in order to decrease the amount of lending exposure to any one borrower.

In the case of bank loans, financing comes directly from banks, rather than purchasers of bonds in the capital markets. The interest expense of bank loans is also often calculated as a variable rate. It is common for bank loans to charge the borrower an interest rate of LIBOR (defined below) plus an additional amount, termed *spread*, which is indicative of the risk associated with the borrower and the seniority of the loan in the case of default. (LIBOR is short for 'London Interbank Offered Rate' and is a daily rate that banks charge to borrow unsecured funds from each other for given periods of time.)

Another important aspect of bank loans is that the lending is frequently syndicated amongst a group of banks in order to decrease the amount of lending exposure to any one borrower. Using this strategy, banks are able to lend money while reducing the risk of bad loan write-downs by lending across a broader range of borrowers. For example, let's say we own a bank. We decide to call it Friends Bank because we have friendly rates. We have a couple of choices regarding lending options:

- **Option 1.** We can lend $100 million to ABC Co and charge an interest expense of LIBOR plus 3.5%.

- **Option 2.** We can lend ABC Co $10 million and get nine other banks to lend ABC Co the remaining $90 million. The rate of interest charged will still be LIBOR plus 3.5%.

As part of option 2, the other banks will also call Friends Bank when they have loans that they want to syndicate out as well. At Friends Bank, we will end up participating as a lender in nine other syndicated loans, which gives the bank a total of ten syndicated loan deals it participates in. All of the loans that we agree to participate in charge an interest rate of LIBOR plus 3.5%. Which option is more attractive?

If you said option number two, you are correct. Under both scenarios, the amount of money earned from interest income is theoretically the same. What makes option number 2 the better option is apparent under a default scenario. In option 1, if ABC Co is unable to pay back its loan, Friends Bank solely takes on all the losses associated with the bad loan. However, under option 2, losses are spread over the ten lending institutions and interest income is still coming in from the other nine borrowers that are current with their interest payments.

In general, bank loans are far more complicated and multi-faceted than bonds. There are several different kinds of bank loans, including term loans, revolving credit facilities, and payment in kind loans, but the important thing to realize is that bank loans can have floating interest rates and often times are syndicated amongst several lenders, whereas bonds are fixed-rate instruments that are sold in the capital markets.

CHAPTER 2

LEVERAGED BUYOUTS: THE PURPOSE

Why do a leveraged buyout? Why would anyone go through the trouble? The answer is quite simple: money. The goal of any LBO transaction is to achieve higher returns on the initial equity investment of the investor. Leveraged buyouts are designed to enhance the returns attainable by equity investors; they do so by decreasing the size of the initial equity investment.

For example, a company is purchased for $100 million with 100% equity and the company is streamlined over the course of a year and later sold for $110 million. The

> The goal of any LBO transaction is to achieve higher returns on the initial equity investment of the investor.

investor just made a 10% return on investment. (Let's ignore the time value of money for now.)

Alternatively, if the investors were able to get a secured loan on the company's assets for $90 million and made an initial equity investment of $10 million, they would still be able to purchase the $100 million company. They would have to pay interest expense on the loan, which happens to be 7% annually. After one year, the investors are able to sell the company for $110 million. With the proceeds from the sale of the company the investors do the following:

- pay down the $90 million loan
- pay $6.3 million in interest expense due.

After paying interest expense and paying back the loan, investors are left with approximately $13.7 million for themselves. That represents a return of about 37%, more than triple the return on equity of the 100% equity transaction!

The bottom line is that leveraged buyouts are about achieving greater returns on equity for investors.

While levered transactions present several advantages to investors, at the same time they bring significant risks. It is the ability of corporations to execute restructuring plans (post LBO) that determine whether a company can sufficiently handle the interest burden taken on as a result of the leveraged buyout and drive the earnings that determine whether greater returns on investment can be realized by investors.

ADVANTAGES OF LEVERAGE

Given that the purpose of leveraged buyouts is to realize greater returns on investment, perhaps it would be useful to examine the several advantages that go hand in hand with leveraged transactions.

The advantages come in a number of diverse forms. Some advantages come in the form of the ability to close transactions while others come in the form of limiting losses. In the end the investor has to make a judgment call as to whether these advantages and the potential for returns are greater than the risks that are also taken on with every transaction.

BIGGER IS POSSIBLE

One of the major advantages of leveraged buyouts is the smaller initial equity investment required to close a transaction. In our example $100 million transaction above, the investor would be required to put up the full $100 million to acquire the company. However, in the case of the leveraged buyout, the investor would only need to hand over $10 million dollars to get the deal done. The other $90 million, we are assuming, could be obtained in the form of a loan secured by the assets of the company being taken over. (We are assuming the company has limited debt prior to any transaction.)

The point is, if the investor did not have $100 million dollars, without leverage the investment would have been out of reach. Leverage allows the transaction to close with only a fraction of the upfront equity commitment. Now an investor can be the proud owner of a $100 million dollar company, even if he only has the ability to invest $10 million.

Alternatively, let's say that the investor does have the $100 million. Rather than tie up the entire $100 million in this one investment, she may want to invest in several different investment opportunities. Using leverage allows her to do that. Our rich investor may wish to invest $10 million in our example opportunity as well as invest in nine other $10 million opportunities. By using leverage, our savvy investor has invested the entire $100 million dollars, but has diversified her risk across several different investments.

LIMITED LOSSES

One of the beauties of equity investing is that you can only lose what you put in. The same truth applies with most leveraged buyouts. One of the main advantages for investors is the limited losses that accompany buying a company mainly with debt secured by the assets of that same company. You can substitute the word 'debt' in this case with 'Other People's Money'.

When an investor is required to commit just 10% of the capital required to purchase a company, it is significantly less than that of the 100% pure equity investor. The potential losses and therefore risk of the pure equity investor are far greater than those of the LBO equity investor. The levered investor has much less capital at risk should the acquired company not succeed. In the case of failure (or bankruptcy), the levered equity investor would almost certainly lose their entire investment, but that would most likely pale in comparison to the total losses realized by a 100% equity investor.

> One of the main advantages for investors is the limited losses that accompany buying a company mainly with debt secured by the assets of that same company.

REDUCED TAXES

Depending on where on the globe you transact, interest expense may be tax deductible. So, while it would be great if money could be borrowed for free and used for LBOs, the consolation is that the tax burden can be reduced based on realized interest expense.

RISKS OF LEVERAGE

For all of its advantages, leverage comes with risk. While it is possible to breakdown the various advantages of leverage into different descriptions the risk of leverage is singular in nature. The risk of leverage is greater default risk.

When times are good and a company is producing earnings to pay its suppliers, employees and officers, leverage is a beautiful thing. However, in times of trouble, when the company is not generating profits, leverage can be a death blow that does not allow a company to get itself back on its feet. Even in times of trouble, interest payments are still required on top of the regular operating expenses that come with operating a company.

> For all of its advantages, leverage comes with risk. The risk of leverage is greater default risk.

The creditors have prepared for the day of failure since before the original credit agreements were signed. In the case of a failing business (or bankruptcy), the creditors stand in line ahead of the equity partners to get their money back. Only after all the creditors get their money back is there any chance of equity investors recouping their investment capital and usually by that time there is nothing left to recoup.

If a company were to not have any debt, but were to fall on tough financial times, the outcome would be somewhat different. The biggest difference would be that there would be less chance of bankruptcy. (We are presuming that there are no unsecured creditors like employees or vendors that have supplied goods or services without being paid.) The company could sell any assets it has on its balance sheet. From the proceeds of the asset sale, the equity partners of the company could keep all the money and help stave off bankruptcy.

Leverage comes with the risk not being able to meet the interest expense obligation. In good times, leverage seems like a wonderful idea. It allows a company to get the most out of the assets on its balance sheet and assists the growth of the company. However, in bad times, the interest burden can weigh on the company so greatly that it becomes a weight around the company's proverbial neck and sinks the company in an ocean of debt.

OUTCOMES

Given what we now know about the advantages and risk associated with leveraged buyouts, let's take a look at a simple example on how a transaction can potentially unfold, for better and then for worse.

In our example we have an investor that has identified a target company for a leveraged takeover. The target company produces essential engine parts for trains and has been doing so, profitably, for nearly 90 years. The target company has very little debt on its balance sheet and strong, steady cash flows. The company has been family owned since its inception and the family is looking to sell 100% of the company.

After conducting his due diligence and analysis the investor calculates a value range for the target company. The analysis, which we will cover in detail later, includes: 1) the market pricing for similar companies as a multiple of EBITDA (Earnings Before Interest Depreciation and Amortization), 2) purchase pricing in previous acquisitions of similar companies, as well as, 3) a discounted cash flow analysis – which also relies on multiples of earnings to derive the implied enterprise value of the company.

The investor carefully analyzes the impact of the target company taking on additional debt and its ability meet the interest payments over a decided time period. From this analysis the investor gains a measure of comfort in the target company's ability to continue to generate earnings, service the debt, and eventually provide a satisfactory return on investment.

Based on his analysis and research, the investor decides to put forth an offer to the current owners of the company. The bid is accepted and the purchase transaction closes successfully at a price of $100 million.

POSITIVE OUTCOME

Now that the leveraged buyout transaction has been completed the hard work begins for those tasked with the job of running the business and ultimately generating earnings. Business managers will focus on operating efficiency and try to identify areas within the company where unnecessary costs can be reduced. They will also try to identify additional revenue-generating opportunities.

The economy continues to grow and businesses are shipping goods by train as much as ever. The company experiences growth in demand for its train engine parts by 5% every year for the next five years. Under these circumstances, the company is able to meet is regular interest payments and realize a return on equity.

As time goes on, the company continues its profitable ways, steadily paying down debt and using its profits to expand operations, which will result in greater revenues and ultimately profits down the road. The company also increases the dividends paid out to owners.

Five years after the original acquisition of the company, our investor decides that he is ready to sell the company. At this point, significant value has been created within the company. Business operations have expanded, and with it, revenue and earnings have also increased. The firm has generated significant positive cash flows that have been used to expand the business and pay the owners, in the form of dividends.

Using the same methodology that was used to value the purchase of the company, the investor is now selling the company at a price that will result in a handsome return on investment. With a large portion of the debt now paid down and turned into equity, our investor is selling a considerably larger portion of the company as equity than he actually bought on the day of purchase. That coupled with the fact that earnings have also grown over the past five years contributes to the returns that the investor expects to realize.

> Five years later, if a large portion of the debt is paid down and turned into equity, an investor can sell a considerably larger portion of the company as equity than he actually bought on the day of purchase.

In the end, our investor identifies a buyer that is willing to purchase the company at the same multiple of EBITDA he purchased the company at. It doesn't sound very exciting at first, but the key facts are that the company's EBITDA has grown 30% over the past five years and while our investor only put up 10% of the purchase price in the form of an initial equity investment, his equity share now accounts for 40% of the company's capital structure. The short summary of this positive outcome is that our investor has made *a lot* of money on this deal by increasing the company's earnings (EBITDA), paying down debt and amassing a larger portion of shareholders' equity in the firm over time.

NEGATIVE OUTCOME

Now that the leveraged buyout transaction has been completed the hard work begins for those tasked with the job of running the business and ultimately generating earnings. Business managers will focus on operating efficiency and try to identify areas within the company where unnecessary costs can be reduced. They will also try to identify additional revenue-generating opportunities.

Faced with a bleak economic horizon, and all of its available cash paying down large interest expenses, a company can find itself in serious trouble.

The greater economy stalls and businesses are not shipping as many goods as they do under normal economic circumstances. The weakening demand for new trains and less expensive alternatives from overseas result in significantly weaker demand for the company's engine parts. Revenues decrease on average by 5%, annually, over the next five years.

The company's cash flow and earnings shrink with the decreasing revenue. The company is faced with difficult decisions – whether, for instance, to make certain capital expenditures, and whether or not to lay off staff. The company is now feeling the weight of the debt burden. All of the company's available cash is going towards paying the large interest expense. Eventually, available cash runs out, the company misses a payment and defaults on its debt.

Faced with a bleak economic horizon and stiff, less expensive competition overseas, the company decides to file for Chapter 7 bankruptcy and is liquidated through the sale of its assets. The lenders are first in line to receive any proceeds from the sale of the company's assets. The company made few capital investments due to economic uncertainty and many of the large corporate assets such as plant property and equipment have approached the end of their useful lives, which translates into the assets fetching very little at the time of sale in bankruptcy. The lenders recoup a portion of the debt they extended the company in the leveraged transaction and the equity investor is wiped out of his original 10% equity investment.

CHAPTER 3

PLAYERS IN A LEVERAGED BUYOUT

INVESTOR

Every LBO starts with the investor. The investor is the individual or private equity group that sees an opportunity and sets the process in motion. They have access to capital for investment and the best way for them to make money is to put the money that they do have to work, in the form of investments. They look for a strong takeover target with small amounts of debt, strong cash flow, assets free for use as collateral, and plenty of room for cost cutting in the current operations. The investors spend lots of time analyzing the potential returns from prospective deals and eventually choose whether to move on a company or not.

The investor is the catalyst behind the transaction. He decides how aggressive or conservative any offer that is put forth to the current

> The investor is motivated to realize the greatest return possible on his investment. This is easier said than done. There are many factors that can affect the outcome.

ownership should be. To a certain extent, the investor also decides how much leverage to use in a transaction. It's only to 'a certain extent' because at points of excessive leverage or non-creditworthy deals the lenders will simply decline to extend credit. The investor also has discretion over the multiple of earnings it is willing to assign as valuation and therefore the purchase price for a company. It is up to the investor to decide what a reasonable valuation and offer price is for a company and it is a decision that must take multiple factors into consideration.

The investor is motivated to ultimately realize the greatest return possible on his investment. This is easier said than done. There are many factors that can affect the outcome. In the most simple sense, it is easier to realize greater returns on equity if that equity is a small number. In an earlier example we demonstrated how an investor could triple the return on investment by using leverage combined with smaller equity investments. However, the investor does not want to saddle the company with such debt that he risks losing his entire investment because of a possible default. For this reason, the investor is motivated to find a balance. The ideal is the greatest amount of debt possible that will not also sink the company down the road, leaving it able to pay down debt, increase earnings and eventually be sold at greater multiple of earnings than it was purchased for.

> The ideal amount of debt is the greatest amount possible that will not also sink the company down the road.

LENDERS - SENIOR BANK DEBT

The banks are one of the major lenders in the leveraged buyout transaction. Typically, banks extend loans that are senior in the credit pecking order and secured by the assets of the company being acquired and sometimes by the assets of the investing company. Banks may participate as syndicated lenders. Under this scenario, as explained in Chapter 1, several banks will come together to lend a portion of the total loan amount. This reduces the credit exposure each bank has to the borrower, while still allowing them to participate as a lender. An investment bank often arranges the syndication, while commercial banks make up a large number of the lenders, along with other investment banks, participating in the syndication as lenders in the deal.

It is the role of the bank to evaluate the projected credit situation of the company post-transaction, and to offer or decline lending terms based on the creditworthiness of the company under the proposed capital structure. This includes the value of the collateral that is being put up to secure the loans. The banks in many respects can function as the breaks in any given transaction by either extending less credit than the investor was originally looking for or by offering lending terms that make the deal less attractive to the investor.

The banks are motivated to assess the risk of lending correctly and set interest rates that are an appropriate reflection of that risk. If a bank does lend, it wants to make sure it is receiving adequate payment for the risks involved.

DEBT INVESTORS - HIGH YIELD

Debt investors are oftentimes the unsecured creditors in the deal and, as a matter of course, command a higher fixed rate of interest, often referred to as high yield, which is compensation for 1) being unsecured and 2) being junior in the credit pecking order to the senior secured bank debt. These creditors find their place in the deal through the purchase of high-yield bonds, which are underwritten and arranged by an investment bank. These creditors are often professional fixed-income investors that understand the risks associated with high-yield corporate bonds.

Similar to the senior secured lenders, the unsecured lender's role is to evaluate the credit quality of the company post-leveraged buyout and determine the risk of the company not being able to pay back its loan. The unsecured lender has to consider the fact that it will only receive its money after the senior secured lender gets paid. In the end the amount of unsecured debt that is issued can make a significant difference in the amount of leverage available in a deal.

> Debt investors are oftentimes the unsecured creditors in the deal and, as a matter of course, command a higher fixed rate of interest, often referred to as high yield.

Unsecured creditors are motivated by the large interest payments that are associated with high-yield bonds. Although unsecured loans used to finance leveraged buyout carry significant risks, ultimately it is the large coupon payments that bring investors forward to purchase the securities once the investment bank issues the bonds. Once again the motivation is a balance between the greed and fear of the creditor, the same two things that run the entire credit markets.

CURRENT OWNERS - SELLERS

The current owners of the company are the people who should know the most about the company, both inside and out. They understand the history and development of the company as well as the operating environment in which they do business. They should also have a keen sense of where the market for their product is heading.

It is up to the owners of the company to consider and ultimately accept or decline offers to sell their ownership in the company. As part of the process, the owners will most likely try to negotiate a larger multiple of earnings into the purchase price. It is the job of the owners to test the upper limits of what the purchasers are willing to pay for ownership in the company and then try to take that offer price a bit further. Business owners will find all sorts of justification for deserving a larger multiple for their earnings; after all, that is what they are supposed to do.

> When a business owner arrives at the decision to sell, there are few greater motivations than, you guessed it – money.

When a business owner arrives at the decision to sell, there are few greater motivations than, you guessed it – money. Although some business owners may also consider such things as the identity of the purchaser, the future of the company post-sale, and the likelihood and degree of cost-cutting after sale, rarely do any of these considerations trump monetary pay-off. It is safe to say that the primary motivation of the business owner is to get the greatest valuation and sale price possible for the business.

If the company has a bright future and growth potential is still relatively high, a savvy owner will demand a greater multiple of earnings for a purchase price before agreeing to sell.

EXISTING CREDITORS

This group of creditors is made up of lenders that issued debt to the company before there was any talk of a leveraged buyout. The existing creditors presumably lent money to the company to help them expand operations or meet liquidity needs or both. Most likely, existing creditors are traditional lenders, such as a commercial bank specializing in making traditional commercial loans. This group likely has a relationship with the company and has a reasonable understanding of the company's credit situation.

The existing lenders do not play a major role in the transaction. They receive the loan principal plus any interest due and pre-payment fees once the leveraged buyout transaction goes through. Generally speaking, institutions that are in the business of making loans like this receive a steady, predictable interest payment on time and leave more exciting affairs to their cousins in the capital markets business. In a situation such as the pre-payment of a bank loan there is typically a pre-payment fee between 1% and 1.5% that is agreed at the initial extending of the loan. The fee is paid to the lender at the time of pre-payment. Once a borrower decides to pre-pay on a loan, the existing lender then becomes focused on seeing that its extended loans and other monies due and receivable are paid back.

> In the event that a lender is large enough, it may be motivated to seek participation as one of the lenders in the leveraged buyout transaction.

In the event that a lender is large enough, it may be motivated to seek participation as one of the lenders in the leveraged buyout transaction. This would present an opportunity for the lender to extended additional loans.

CHAPTER 4

ANATOMY OF A PRACTITIONER'S ANALYSIS

OVERVIEW OF FINANCIAL STATEMENTS

F inancial statements are the lifeblood of all corporate financial analysis. Historical financials are analyzed to understand the history, growth and earnings performance of the company. By looking at a company's historical performance via financial statements, certain operating ratios can be identified that help give an indication of where the company is headed. These include things such as inventory turnover as well as revenue growth trends. Once trends are identified they can be used to help form reasonable assumptions for projecting future performance in the form of pro forma financials.

Pro forma financial statements are used to make a reasonable approximation of where financial analysts think a company may be headed. Typically, this includes some assumptions about the rate at which revenue will grow in the future as well as any expected changes in the company's expenses.

> By looking at a company's historical performance via financial statements, certain operating ratios can be identified that help give an indication of where the company is headed.

Particularly in the case of leveraged buyouts, analysis is focused on projecting out changes in the company's capital structure, namely an increased amount of debt, and the financial cost that are associated with it. Pro forma financial statements are a combination of historical trends and reasonable assumptions about how a company will perform in the future. Assumptions should be grounded in reasonable logic and be able to stand up against scrutiny.

Ultimately, the balance sheet, income statement, and cash flow statement work together to explain the performance of a company. None of the statements is independent of the others and they must be understood individually in order to comprehend financial performance as a whole. Once the purpose and meaning of each financial statement is understood, a meaningful analysis can be assembled.

BALANCE SHEET

The balance sheet captures the assets of the company, which includes cash and cash that should be on its way (receivables) as well as assets that should be used to generate revenue for the company. This includes things like equipment, patents, land, etc.

> Ultimately, the balance sheet, income statement, and cash flow statement work *together* to explain the performance of a company. None of the statements is independent of the others.

The other side of the balance sheet is made up of liabilities and shareholders' equity. You can think about this as the way the company funds itself.

In the case of a leveraged buyout, the right side of a balance sheet would typically see a large shift in the amount of debt relative to equity. The assets of the company would not necessarily change immediately after a leveraged buyout, as the transaction is primarily a matter of the company's capital structure. The cash that the company generates via its business activities in the future can be used to pay down debt and increase shareholders' equity through retained earnings.

INCOME STATEMENT

The income statement reflects the earnings of the company over a period of time. What's just as important is the fact that even though the income statement is a reflection of the company's ability to generate earnings over time, it includes both cash and non-cash expenses, such as depreciation and amortization, and for this reason the total net income for the period is almost never the amount of money actually generated or realized by a company over that time period. For that you would have to look at the cash flow statement. However, the income statement is a critical tool for evaluating the earnings performance of a company by taking into consideration the revenue and all cash and non-cash expenses associated with running the company. Last but not least, Earnings Before Interest, Taxes, Depreciation and Amortization (EBITDA) is derived from the income statement and is widely used in valuation and comparable companies analysis when trying to triangulate corporate valuation.

CASH FLOW STATEMENT

The cash flow statement reflects the actual amount of cash that comes in and goes out of a company. The cash flow statement is generally broken up into three sections: cash flow derived from the company's operations, cash flow from investments the company makes, and cash flow from any financing in the form of, for example, debt (inflow) or share issuance (inflow) / repurchases (outflow).

Any loans/debt the company takes on appears as a cash inflow in the financing section of the cash flow statement. With leveraged buyouts, we are particularly concerned with the cash flow available to pay down debt, as an investor will want to know (among other things) to what degree the company can pay down money borrowed to purchase it.

> With leveraged buyouts, we are particularly concerned with the cash flow available to pay down debt.

DEBT SWEEP

Speaking of paying down debt … While not one of the financial statements, a debt sweep is used alongside the financial statements to project or track the paydown of debt with excess cash, which reduces the debt balance on the balance sheet and also affects the amount of interest expense due each period, depending on the amount of debt paid down. The debt sweep is an integral part of every leveraged buyout analysis and intertwines into every aspect of the financial statements. There is often a pre-payment fee for the early paydown of senior debt. This is frequently a 1–1.5% charge on the principal amount that is being paid down early.

APPLICATION OF FINANCIAL STATEMENTS

Financial analysis, at a high level, can be broken down into two phases – 1) historical and 2) forecasted. The historical portion of leveraged buyout analysis is focused on extracting current and historical annual (or quarterly) data from the financial statements of the company. This information can be found in the annual or quarterly reports of the company. In the US, these financial reports are filed with the Securities and Exchange Commission and are referred to as the 10-K and 10-Q, respectively.

Before bringing the historical financial information into your analysis, you will want to make sure that your spreadsheet is set up in a layout that is conducive to your analysis. In other words, set up your analysis with a layout that you are comfortable with and that you feel is easiest to highlight the material points of your analysis. In practice, this could take the form of consolidating line items for the company's different types of inventory and having one line item, 'Inventory'. You would do this because having several different line items for various types of inventory does not do anything other than clutter your analysis. Ultimately, your analysis should be set up in such a way that it makes it easier to formulate and present your analysis, whether it takes the form of rearranging the order of data presented in a financial statement or consolidating line items of data.

Once your leveraged buyout analysis layout is in place, it is time to bring in the historical financial information of the company. For the purposes of easy delineation between formulas and direct entry numbers, including assumptions, in the spreadsheet, be sure to distinguish direct number entries in your spreadsheet with a unique color, typically blue. This will help later in your analysis when you wish to change an assumption or edit a cell with a formula in it.

INCOME STATEMENT

The income statement leads off our LBO analysis. From the income statement we look at the historical revenue and cost figures of the company to identify trends and form assumptions about the annual growth rate for revenue as well as the cost structure of the company. The assumptions that are formed based on analyzing the historical income statement will be used to forecast projected revenue production and operating costs in the future. Cost assumptions made as a percentage of revenue will directly translate into projected operating margins for the company. These items along with taxes will have a major influence on the projected growth and profitability of the company in our analysis. Revenue growth and all cash expenses will also affect the company's ability to generate cash to meet interest payments and pay down outstanding debt.

The growth and value of any company begins with revenue. If revenue begins to decrease, a company has little choice but to look for areas to cut costs. However, costs can only be reduced to a certain

> Ideally, a company will have strong and stable revenues (which will lead to strong, steady cash flow). Opportunities for cost reductions within its operations are also prized.

point. For this reason, analysts will pay close attention to the revenue of any potential buyout target. Ideally, a company will have strong and stable revenues (which will lead to strong, steady cash flow). Additionally, it is also looked on favorably when a potential buyout company has opportunities for cost reductions within its operations. Investors and business managers see this as a proven way to increase the profitability of a company that can later turn into handsome returns for investors upon the sale of the company.

BALANCE SHEET

If the income statement speaks to the fuel of the company's growth (i.e. revenue and earnings), the balance sheet provides all gauges that report on the health of the engine. Any reported balance sheet is only a snapshot of a company's financial condition. So by looking at the balance sheet we know what the current financial condition of that company is *at that point in time*. Typically, major line items to take note of on the lefthand side of the balance sheet would be cash and other current assets, particularly any revenue-generating assets. On the righthand side or the liabilities side of the balance sheet we would be want to take note of current liabilities and all other interest-bearing liabilities, as well as shareholders' equity.

The righthand, or liability, side of the balance sheet is particularly important in a leveraged buyout, because the analyst needs to assess potential capital structures and make a determination as to whether the target company can withstand the financial pressures that go along with a leveraged buyout. The interest expense that accompanies the debt is calculated from the beginning debt balance of each period and appears in the income statement as interest expense. In times of profitability excess cash is used to pay down the outstanding principal on the debt. This in turn works to reduce the interest expense due each following period.

In short, the balance sheet records the levels of debt the company keeps on its books, which translates into the interest expense that embodies the financial burden of a leveraged buyout.

CASH FLOW STATEMENT

There is an expression, 'numbers don't lie'. That expression loses some validity to a normal person off the street when you show them an income statement filled with what are known as non-cash charges or value assets on a balance sheet at $1 million when the most you could expect to sell the asset for in the open market is somewhere near $0.

> In the case of the cash flow statement, the numbers don't lie – or at least they shouldn't.

(Note: The practice of reflecting assets on the balance sheet at prices that represent what the assets could be sold for on the open market is referred to as *marking to market*.)

Fortunately, in the case of the cash flow statement, the numbers don't lie – or at least they shouldn't lie. The cash flow statement is used to determine the actual amount of cash that came into or flowed out of the company. It should strip out any non-cash expenses such as depreciation and amortization and include things like cash spent on capital expenditures or changes in net working capital. This way it will provide a genuine reflection of any increase or decrease in cash.

The cash flow statement is extremely important in the case of a leveraged buyout analysis because it is cash that is used to make interest payments and pay down principal on existing debt. Cash flow from the company's operations, as described above, is forecasted out along with the other financial statements to determine the amount of cash flow available each period to pay down debt. The cash flow and ability of the company to pay down debt is at the heart of the leveraged buyout analysis and cannot be overemphasized.

DEBT SWEEP

The debt sweep is used in conjunction with the cash flow statement to determine and project the amount of leverage the company retains on its balance sheet. As we pointed

> The debt sweep is the epicenter of all reduction or raising of debt on the balance sheet.

out for the cash flow statement, cash available to pay down existing debt is calculated based on net income after adding back non-cash charges and adjusting for considerations such as capital expenditures and changes in net working capital. The resulting number is used within the debt sweep to determine to what degree existing leverage can be paid down or in the case of a negative result, the additional cash the company must borrow to fund its operations.

The debt sweep is where all calculations regarding changes in leverage occur. It is the epicenter of all reduction or raising of debt on the company's balance sheet and is inseparable from the cash flow statement. The resulting calculations in the debt sweep will have a direct impact on the interest expense of the following period. The more cash generated, the more debt can be paid down. The more debt can be paid down, the lower the interest expense that will be charged at the end of the period. The debt sweep captures the movement of debt on the balance sheet and plays a critical role in calculating the levels of debt on which interest may be charged for upcoming periods.

RATIO ANALYSIS

Ratio analysis is used to measure the performance and financial health of a company at a given point in time. Often times, ratios are used to compare one company against several comparable companies to get a sense of how a company is performing relative to its peers. Common areas for analysis via ratios include profitability (return on assets, and return on equity), capital structure and leverage (debt to equity), and credit (EBITDA to interest expense or EBIT to interest expense).

Ratios should be used and analyzed within in the context of the financial statements and other ratios. On a standalone basis, one ratio seldom provides a significant amount of insight on a particular company. However, when viewed within the context of a company's financial statements and performance in terms of absolute dollars (or pounds, or euros), ratios can provide meaningful insight into the workings and performance of a company, particularly when comparing across firms with varying scales of operation.

LBO ANALYSIS

GOALS OF LBO ANALYSIS

When putting an LBO analysis together, the first question that should be asked is – What am I trying to accomplish with this analysis?

The simple answer is that the goal of the analysis is to forecast the returns of the investment. However, there are several other aspects of the potential transaction that an investor will be interested in knowing about before making the decision to invest. In general, a potential investor will want to know more about the *path* that is being taken on the way to the projected return on investment.

Cash in hand

For instance, as part of the analysis one of the goals should be to identify how much debt can be regularly paid down based on the pro forma operational cash flow of the company. This information will be very important to any potential investor. Firstly, accelerated debt repayment means decreased interest expense. Secondly, and perhaps more importantly, it also means that the company will have some financing options in the event the market takes a turn for the worse. For example, if the company has paid down a large portion of its debt and needs additional financing for whatever reason, it will be able to receive additional financing using the company's assets as collateral – just as was done with the original leveraged buyout of the firm. This option would not be available to the company if all if its assets were already being used as collateral on outstanding debt. For this reason, understanding a company's ability and timeliness to pay down debt also gives an indication of future financing flexibility.

In the event a company is struggling to make ends meet and has exhausted all its options as far as debt financing is concerned, one of the options the company is left with is issuing additional equity. Whether or not the company can find an interested equity investor is a different story; it will be completely dependent on the individual circumstances of the situation. However, what is consistent across all new equity issuances is that investors see their ownership stake in a company get diluted with the sale of new equity, which is why in many cases the issuance of new equity is the measure of last resort.

For that reason, investors like to use the LBO analysis to see whether a predictably strong, steady pay down of leverage is possible from the earliest years of an

> Investors like to use LBO analysis to see whether a predictably strong, steady pay down of leverage is possible from the earliest years.

investment. A strong and steady paydown of debt will give the owners of the company both options in bad times and lower their interest expense in the future. These items are central in the consideration of a leveraged buyout. Debt levels and the ability to paydown debt should be clearly highlighted in an LBO analysis. A complete analysis should provide an indication of the target company's ability to pay down excess leverage under assumed scenarios.

Feeling sensitive

Another goal of any good LBO analysis should be to address the various scenarios that can affect investor returns. Indeed, every financial analysis begins with a base of assumptions and results in outcomes that project how a company will perform if things turn out as planned. However, things rarely turn out as planned. This simple truth can be acknowledged in your analysis by using scenarios.

One commonly used method of analyzing outcomes under different scenarios is called sensitivity analysis. Generally, sensitivity analysis uses the table function in MS Excel to calculate various outcomes that occur within a range of differing assumption inputs. As you will see in our example analysis, we use the table function to create a sensitivity analysis for the Year 5 IRR (internal rate of return) under differing Exit EBITDA multiples as well as differing levels of initial equity investment. By doing this, an analysis can cover a broad range of possibilities and provide valuable insight to investors as they contemplate a potential investment.

*   *   *

While the primary goal of a leveraged buyout analysis is to forecast the returns of the potential investment, there are several pieces of information that are important to examine and understand. Given the highly leveraged nature of the transaction and the risks that are associated with it, it is important to pay heightened attention to the debt levels of the company. You will also want to be sure to account for any potential variation in the assumptions built into your analysis. This will provide a greater insight into how an investment's returns can be affected by changes in the given variables. It is important to highlight these points in your analysis as they examine significant risks taken on by any investor.

STEPS IN CREATING AN LBO ANALYSIS

1. DETERMINE THE SOURCES AND USES OF FUNDS FOR THE TRANSACTION

In the very beginning we need to determine how much the leveraged buyout is going to cost and how it is going to get paid for.

In order to determine how much a transaction is going to cost, our starting point is the company's current stock price. On top of a current stock price a premium is often added to sweeten the deal and convince the current shareholders to sell. The result is the offered acquisition price. Multiply the offered price by the number of shares outstanding and you have the total cost of the acquired equity. On top of the cost of the acquired equity there will be transaction costs for bankers, lawyers and the like that will require payment as well. Finally, any existing net debt, which is made up of interest-bearing debt less cash on the balance sheet, will often times be refinanced and hence require cash to be paid down. All in all, the total use of funds (or cash required to close the transaction) will be the sum of the acquisition equity, associated transaction costs, and net debt that is refinanced:

```
cash to close the deal = acquisition equity + associated
transaction costs + net debt refinanced
```

With the price tag for the transaction fully established we need to determine where the money is going to come from to pay for the transaction. In the end, the investor has to make a decision as to how much equity will be put up in the buyout. This is often influenced by a sensitivity analysis on various financing options and how much creditors are willing to lend. In many cases the equity partners are willing to take as much leverage as they can get from creditors and risk as little of their own capital as possible. Once the equity investment amount is determined, the debt financing will account for the balance of the required funds for the transaction. Note that there can be more than one debt instrument used to finance a leveraged buyout and each separate type of debt financing will charge its own interest rate based on several factors, including seniority in the credit structure.

2. FORECAST THE PRO FORMA INCOME STATEMENT

The income statement analysis begins by looking at the past performance of the company. Past performance is used to estimate what revenue growth and cost structures will look like in the future. Revenue drives the overall growth of a company. Assumptions are made about the annual growth rate of revenue for the company. These growth rates are typically based on the past

> Past performance is used to estimate what revenue growth and cost structures will look like in the future.

revenue growth of the company and other factors, such as the larger economy or the growth prospects for the industry the company competes in.

Similar to revenue, most costs estimates are formulated and heavily based on the previous performance of the company. There are several methods for estimating pro forma costs. One common method is forecasting costs as a percentage of revenue. This method increases costs in direct proportion to the growth of the business and its revenues. This method works well with items such as cost of goods sold and to some extent selling, general and administrative, although some may prefer another method. Some costs such as depreciation and amortization can be determined by using more complex methods and amortization schedules. (More complex treatment of depreciation and amortization is beyond the scope of this book, so for the purposes of focusing on leveraged buyout analysis we assume in our example that depreciation and amortization grow as a percentage of revenue as well.)

> There are several methods for estimating pro forma costs. One common method is forecasting costs as a percentage of revenue.

Prior year interest expense can be ignored because it is not a concern when formulating a pro forma income statement, as we will be calculating interest expense based on a new capital structure with a separate interest rate. However, interest income and interest expense cannot be calculated until pro forma cash flow and debt paydown have been estimated. This means that the interest portion of the income statement must be revisited later in the creation phase of the analysis in order to be completed.

3. CALCULATE PRO FORMA CASH FLOW

Cash is one of the most important items on every corporate balance sheet. The change in cash for each period is tracked via the cash flow statement. A traditional cash flow statement is composed of three sections: 1) cash flow from operations, 2) cash flow from investing, and 3) cash flow from financing activities. However, in the case of a leveraged buyout we are concerned with the amount of cash that can be used to pay down debt over the course of the forecast period. For this reason, the cash flow analysis of an LBO will focus on cash flow available for debt repayment. This translates into cash flow after operating and investing activities. Depreciation is added back to net income; changes in net working capital are accounted for and any capital expenditures are subtracted from the available cash amount. The resulting figure is the cash flow available to pay down debt for the period.

4. CALCULATE CHANGES AND PAYDOWN OF LEVERAGE VIA THE DEBT SWEEP ANALYSIS

We use a debt sweep to help calculate how much debt should be paid down during each period based on a few factors. Begin with the debt amount that the company took on as part of the leveraged buyout transaction. This should include all interest-bearing debt that the company has on its balance sheet. The amount of debt paid down each period will depend on 1) the cash flow amount available for debt repayment and 2) the amount of debt remaining on the company's balance sheet each period.

Frequently in a leveraged buyout analysis it is assumed that the entire amount of cash flow available for the repayment of debt is used for that purpose when the amount of debt is greater than the available cash flow figure. Under circumstances where the period's available cash flow amount is greater than the existing debt on the company's balance sheet the excess cash is presumed to be added to the ending cash balance on the balance sheet. In other words the cash balance of the company increases when the cash flow available for debt repayment is larger than the existing debt on the company's balance sheet.

Both the interest expense and interest income the company recognizes in its income statement are calculated based on the debt and cash calculations that result from the debt sweep. This is the heart of the leveraged buyout. The success of the company depends on its ability to pay down its debt. This determines whether or not a transaction can emerge as a profitable endeavor for the investors or result in the company drowning in its own debt.

5. DETERMINE EXPECTED RETURNS AND MULTIPLES OF CAPITAL

On completing the debt sweep and cash portion of the analysis it is time to calculate expected returns. The internal rate of return (IRR) is calculated for each period of the explicit forecast range to get a sense of how profitable the investment is expected to be. Multiply each period's calculated EBITDA figure by an assumed exit EBITDA multiple to determine the implied enterprise value of the firm. Exit EBITDA multiples are oftentimes a number that is close to the multiples of comparable companies. (It is also logical that, all things being equal, the exit multiple would not be too different from the original buyout multiple.) Subtract the company's net debt for each period from the respective implied enterprise value and you are left with the implied equity value. We do this because the implied equity figure is what will be used to calculate the investment's implied IRR. Remember that we are comparing the initial equity investment with the amount of money the investor would receive upon the sale of their ownership in the company.

In addition to the internal rate of return, it is common to calculate the implied multiple of money for an investment. Divide implied equity value by the initial equity investment amount to arrive at the multiple value for each period. Unlike the IRR calculation, the implied multiple of money does not take into consideration the time value of money. However, the implied multiple of money does deal in terms of absolute dollars, which makes it easy to quickly grasp how much money the investor expects to realize in returns.

6. CALCULATE SHAREHOLDERS' EQUITY AND RELEVANT CREDIT RATIOS AND STATISTICS

Ratios can be calculated as a means of measuring the performance and health of the company. Ratios and statistics are useful tools as they facilitate not only the measuring of a company's financial health, but also the comparing of different companies on a relative basis.

Ratios and statistics help us measure a company's financial health and compare different companies on a relative basis.

Some statistics that would be of interest in a leveraged buyout analysis focus on the capital structure and credit ratios of the company. This may include ratios such as, debt to equity, debt to capital, EBITDA to interest, EBIT to interest, debt to EBITDA, and net debt to EBITDA to name a few. Ratios should be calculated for all periods within the explicit forecast range. When completed, the ratios should help in identifying any trends or patterns occurring within the company.

7. SENSITIVITY ANALYSIS

Finally, we can conduct a sensitivity analysis on the expected returns of the investment based on varying amounts of initial equity investment and exit EBITDA multiples. This is a great means of wrapping up the contemplated investment analysis by providing a range of anticipated returns under different circumstances.

PART II

BUILDING AN ANALYSIS

OVERVIEW OF AN ANALYSIS

Building a leveraged buyout model, as with any financial analysis, is about organization and proper structure. There is a certain order to the steps in building an analysis that flows naturally and allows the reader of the analysis to quickly take in the information and make sense of all the numbers on the page. In this part of the book we will walk through the creation of a basic leveraged buyout transaction. By the end of this example explanation you should feel comfortable with all the key aspects of an LBO model and know how to construct one on your own.

THE STEPS AHEAD

The first step in building the analysis is preparing the sources and uses of funds for the leveraged buyout. After that, we will calculate and build out projections into the income statement. For our purposes, the best way to do this is by using some basic revenue growth and per-cent-of-margins assumptions.

After we have completed this work on the income statement we can focus our attention on the always important cash flows of the company as well as a debt sweep analysis, which breaks down the details regarding the paydown of debt that the company will be carrying on its balance sheet.

After we have finished analyzing the company's cash flow and leverage, we can then calculate returns to shareholders, as well as something called the multiples of capital.

Once we have completed all of this we will look at what the effects will be, based on the scenario that we have projected, on shareholders' equity as well as the company's credit statistics.

	A	B	C	D	E	F	G	H	I	J
1	**ABC Company**									
2	**Sources and Uses of Cash**									
3	*(Dollars in millions)*									
4										
5	Uses of Funds									
6	Acquisition Equity					$ 16,200				
7	Net Debt Refinanced					10				
8	Total Transaction Costs					100				
9	Total Uses of Funds					$ 16,310				
10										
11	Sources of Funds									
12	New Equity					$ 4,500				
13	New Debt					11,810				
14	Total Sources of Funds					$ 16,310				
15										
16						1/1/11				
17	Current Stock Price					$ 25.00				
18	Acquisition Premium					20.0%				
19	Acquisition Stock Price					$ 30.00				
20	Shares Outstanding [1]					540				
21										
22	Transaction Enterprise Value					$ 16,210				
23	TEV as a Multiple of Year 0									
24	Revenue					0.8x				
25	EBITDA					8.6x				
26	(1) Use diluted shares outstanding via treasury method whenever applicable.									
27										
28										
29	**ABC Company**									
30	**Income Statement**									
31	*(Dollars in millions)*									
32							Pro Forma			
33					Year 0	Year 1	Year 2	Year 3	Year 4	Year 5
34	Net Revenue				$20,000	$21,400	$22,898	$24,501	$26,216	$28,051
35										
36	Expenses									
37	Cost of Goods Sold				12,300	13,161	14,082	15,068	16,123	17,251
38	Selling, General and Administrative				6,200	6,634	7,098	7,595	8,127	8,696
39	Other and Misc.				20	20	20	20	20	20
40	Total Expenses				18,520	19,815	21,201	22,683	24,270	25,967
41										
42	Operating Income				1,480	1,585	1,697	1,818	1,946	2,084
43	Interest Expense				-531	-531	-515	-495	-473	-447
44	Interest Income				13	13	13	13	13	13
45	Pre-Tax Income				961	1,066	1,195	1,335	1,486	1,649
46	Taxes				-336	-373	-418	-467	-520	-577
47	Net Income				$ 625	$ 693	$ 777	$ 868	$ 966	$ 1,072
48										
49	EBITDA				$ 1,880	$ 2,013	$ 2,155	$ 2,308	$ 2,471	$ 2,645
50	*EBITDA Margin*				*9.4%*	*9.4%*	*9.4%*	*9.4%*	*9.4%*	*9.4%*
51										
52	Revenue Growth Rate (Annual)					7.0%	7.0%	7.0%	7.0%	7.0%
53										
54	Depreciation and Amortization				$400	$428	$458	$490	$524	$561
55										
56	Percentage of Revenue									
57	Cost of Goods Sold				61.5%	61.5%	61.5%	61.5%	61.5%	61.5%
58	Selling, General and Administrative				31.0%	31.0%	31.0%	31.0%	31.0%	31.0%
59	Depreciation and Amortization				2.0%	2.0%	2.0%	2.0%	2.0%	2.0%
60										
61	Tax Rate				35.0%	35.0%	35.0%	35.0%	35.0%	35.0%
62										
63										
64										
65	**IRR Analysis**									
66	*(Dollars in millions)*									
67							Pro Forma			
68						Year 1	Year 2	Year 3	Year 4	Year 5
69	Exit EBITDA Multiple			8.0x						
70	Implied Enterprise Value					$ 16,104	$ 17,242	$ 18,461	$ 19,764	$ 21,159
71	Less: Net Debt					(10,938)	(10,505)	(10,005)	(9,432)	(8,781)
72	Implied Equity Value					$ 5,166	$ 6,738	$ 8,456	$ 10,332	$ 12,378
73										
74	Implied IRR					14.8%	22.4%	23.4%	23.1%	22.4%
75	Implied Multiple of Capital					1.1x	1.5x	1.9x	2.3x	2.8x

K	L	M	N	O	P	Q	R	S	T	U

ABC Company
Cash Flow and Debt Sweep Analysis
(Dollars in millions)

			Pro Forma				
		Year 0	Year 1	Year 2	Year 3	Year 4	Year 5
Net Income			$ 693	$ 777	$ 868	$ 966	$ 1,072
Depreciation			428	458	490	524	561
Capital Expenditures			(428)	(458)	(490)	(524)	(561)
Change in Net Working Capital (1.5% Rev)		1.5%	(321)	(343)	(368)	(393)	(421)
Cash Flow for Debt Repayments			$ 372	$ 433	$ 500	$ 573	$ 651
Debt Balance							
Beginning Balance	Rate	4.5%	$ 11,810	$ 11,438	$ 11,005	$ 10,505	$ 9,932
Borrowing / (Paydown)			(372)	(433)	(500)	(573)	(651)
Ending Balance		$ 11,810	$ 11,438	$ 11,005	$ 10,505	$ 9,932	$ 9,281
Cash Balance							
Beginning Balance	Rate	2.5%	$ 500	$ 500	$ 500	$ 500	$ 500
Additions			-	-	-	-	-
Ending Balance		3.50%	$ 500	$ 500	$ 500	$ 500	$ 500

ABC Company
Shareholders' Equity

		Year 0	Year 1	Year 2	Year 3	Year 4	Year 5
Beginning Balance			$ 4,400	$ 5,093	$ 5,870	$ 6,737	$ 7,703
Plus: Net Income			693	777	868	966	1,072
Ending Balance		$ 4,400	$ 5,093	$ 5,870	$ 6,737	$ 7,703	$ 8,775

Ratios Analysis

	Year 1	Year 2	Year 3	Year 4	Year 5
Total Debt / EBITDA	6.3x	5.7x	5.1x	4.6x	4.0x	3.5x
Net Debt / EBITDA	6.0x	5.4x	4.9x	4.3x	3.8x	3.3x
EBITDA / Interest	3.5x	3.8x	4.2x	4.7x	5.2x	5.9x
EBIT / Interest	2.8x	3.0x	3.3x	3.7x	4.1x	4.7x
Total Debt / Equity	2.7x	2.2x	1.9x	1.6x	1.3x	1.1x
Total Debt / Capital	72.9%	69.2%	65.2%	60.9%	56.3%	51.4%

5 Year IRR- Sensitivity Analysis

			New Equity Injection			
	22.4%	$ 3,500	$ 4,000	$ 4,500	$ 5,000	$ 5,500
Exit	6.0x	11.1%	10.2%	9.5%	8.9%	8.4%
EBITDA	7.0x	19.6%	18.0%	16.7%	15.6%	14.6%
Multiple	8.0x	26.2%	24.2%	22.4%	21.0%	19.7%
	9.0x	31.7%	29.3%	27.3%	25.6%	24.1%
	10.0x	36.4%	33.7%	31.5%	29.5%	27.9%

Snapshot of the completed analysis

CHAPTER 5

HOW MUCH AND WHO'S PAYING FOR IT?

his chapter is concerned with those stages in the analysis where we work out how much a buyout will cost (uses of funds), where the money to pay for this might come from (sources of funds and leverage), and gauging whether a deal offers good value or not. This example is explained from a practitioner's point of view, using MS Excel – just as it would be created in a professional setting. Templates and example models can be found at **www.fin-models.com**.

USES OF FUNDS

PRICE

We begin our analysis by entering the ABC Company's **current stock price** of $25.00 in cell (F17).

In order to entice the current shareholders of ABC Co. to sell the stock, we assume that there is a **transaction premium** of 20% (F18) that will be paid.

The rationale here is simple: as the current stock owner you will sell the stock if you think the premium price is above what the stock is really worth. If you think the stock is worth more than what is being offered and for whatever reason it is not being reflected in the market (plus premium) price, you would not accept the offer.

The objective of the would-be purchaser of the stock is to purchase the equity at a price that is less than what the company will later be sold for post restructuring. We can make it more complicated than that, but there's no need to here.

It is worth mentioning that herein lies the danger of bidding wars. When two separate would-be purchasers of a stock emerge and attempt to outbid each other, each time increasing the price of their offers, each increased bid decreases any future returns and increases any future losses! This is the reason that purchasers *must* perform rigorous analysis prior to any bids being submitted for consideration.

Our **acquisition stock price** of $30.00 (F19) can be determined by multiplying the **current stock price** (F18) by (1+F19), the **transaction premium**.

◇	A	B	C	D	E	F
1	ABC Company					
2	Sources and Uses of Cash					
3	(Dollars in millions)					
4						
5	Uses of Funds					
6	Acquisition Equity					$16,200
7	Net Debt Refinanced					10
8	Total Transaction Costs					100
9	Total Uses of Funds					$16,310
10						
11	Sources of Funds					
12	New Equity					$4,500
13	New Debt					11,810
14	Total Sources of Funds					$16,310
15						
16						1/1/11
17	Current Stock Price					$25.00
18	Acquisition Premium					20.0%
19	Acquisition Stock Price					$30.00
20	Shares Outstanding [1]					540
21						
22	Transaction Enterprise Value					$16,210
23	TEV as a Multiple of Year 0					
24	Revenue					0.8x
25	EBITDA					8.6x
26	(1) Use diluted shares outstanding via treasury method whenever applicable.					

Sources and uses of cash

NUMBER OF SHARES

The next item that we should bring into our model is the **number of shares outstanding**. This number can be found in the company's 10-K or annual report.

This is a good time to mention the concept of fully diluted shares outstanding. Fully diluted shares outstanding is the number of common shares that would be outstanding if all instruments that can be converted to common equity, such as options, were converted. Fully diluted number of shares is calculated via the Treasury Method, which adds new shares from converted options, less any shares that are assumed to be purchased back by the company in the open market using the proceeds from the converted options. The notion of fully diluted shares outstanding is important because it is the number that any analyst will most likely consider when conducting a valuation analysis on a per-share basis.

For the purposes of this discussion we are solely concerned with the fundamentals of LBO analysis and therefore will not muddy the waters with convertible instruments in this discussion. Instead we will assume that the number of shares outstanding, found in the annual report, is 540,000,000 and there are no equity options or other convertibles securities outstanding.

Let's take inventory of what we know so far. We know:

1. the current stock price

2. the premium that we are willing to pay (and hence acquisition price per share)

3. the total number of shares outstanding.

ACQUISITION EQUITY

Now that we know these items, we can figure out how much money is going to be required to purchase the equity of the company. The purchase of the company's equity will be a major use of funds in the leveraged buyout of the company. In our example, we will refer to this item as **acquisition equity** (F6). To calculate acquisition equity you multiple the acquisition stock price by the number of shares outstanding.

NET DEBT

The other major use of funds to consider in your LBO analysis is the purchase of the target company's **net debt** (F7). In our example, the net debt is the sum of short-term debt ($50 million) + current portion of long-term debt ($500 million) + long-term debt ($3,960 million) - the cash on the company's balance sheet ($5,000 million). All of these figures can be found on the target company's latest balance sheet.

Note: In your calculation of **net debt** to be refinanced (F7), do not subtract the entire cash balance from total debt outstanding unless you want to have zero cash on the books post-transaction. Instead, decide on the amount of cash you wish the company to carry on its books post-LBO and use that number to decrease your cash component in the calculation of net debt to be refinanced. In our example model, we have assumed a cash figure of $500 million.

ABC Company	
Net Debt Calculation	
(Dollars in millions)	
	Year 0
Short-Term Debt	$ 50
Current Portion of LT Debt	500
Long-Term Debt	3,960
Minus: Total Cash	-5,000
Plus: Cash Left on BS	500
Net Debt	$ 10

Net debt calculation

TRANSACTION COSTS

The final item that we will consider in our example as a use of funds will be the **transaction costs**. This cost will include the fees that are paid to the attorneys, advisors, brokers and all other parties that are involved in some way with the transaction.

For our purposes, we will assume that the total costs associated with completing the transaction are $100 million. However, you could approximate these costs by gathering information on previous comparable transactions that were done to get some idea of what it would cost to complete the transaction and then make a reasonable assumption based on the research that was conducted.

TOTAL USE OF FUNDS

If we sum all the uses of funds that we laid out for the contemplated transaction we see that the leveraged buyout will require approximately $16 billion (F9) to be completed. This figure is the sum of the acquisition equity, the company's current equity stake plus premium, the net debt to be refinanced, and the total transaction costs. These items combined give us the LBO's **total use of funds**.

SOURCES OF FUNDS

We just figured out how we are going to spend the money – now we need to figure out how we are going to get the money! This is after all an LBO, so why don't we discuss how we are going to finance the transaction? Another way of saying this is *sources of funds*.

As you may have guessed, sources of funds are made up of the various types of capital used to complete the transaction. We will also see that different types of source charge varying prices for the use of their capital. This is is largely dependent upon how high or low a source sits in the totem pole of credit seniority.

> Different sources charge different prices for their funds – it comes down to 'seniority'.

For the purposes of simplicity and focusing on the fundamentals of how to conduct LBO analysis, let's assume that the total amount of **equity capital** that the equity investors are willing to put at risk in this deal is $4,500 million. This number was derived based on the risk appetite of the equity investors and careful consideration of a sensitivity analysis, which we will take a look at later in this book.

LEVERAGING UP

So far we have determined 1) How much money the transaction is going to cost to complete (F9); and 2) How much equity we are willing to put into the deal (E12). The gap that exists between those two numbers is the amount of someone else's money that we are going to use to complete the transaction. In other words, we are going to borrow the difference between the total use of funds and the equity source of funds in order to bridge the gap between the money that we have and the money that we need to purchase the target company.

As you may have noticed, when we take a look at our sources of funds, the debt portion is more than double the amount of equity that is being used in the deal. This heavy reliance on debt financing or leverage to acquire the target is the meaning behind the name leveraged buyout.

TRANSACTION ENTERPRISE VALUE – MEASURING VALUE

Transaction enterprise value (TEV) is the sum of the acquisition equity, which we already calculated in cell (F6), and the existing net debt refinanced (F7). TEV can be thought of as the amount of money that is required purely for the leveraged buyout of the business, without taking into consideration the cost of doing the transaction (i.e. attorneys' fees, bankers' fees, etc.). In our example, if we add the acquisition value and the existing net debt refinanced, this gives us a TEV of $16,210 million (F22).

A similar example outside of the LBO world would be the purchase of a house. The amount of money required to purchase a house is not only the price of the house, but also includes closing fees, which are subject to negotiation.

Why do we care about transaction enterprise value? As a standalone number, TEV does not tell us much regarding whether or not the price of the buyout is of good value. In fact, about the only thing that we can determine from this number is whether or not the price is within or out of reach, depending on the financing resources we believe to be available.

In order to better understand the relative value concerning the contemplated transaction we will look at the transaction enterprise value as a multiple of revenue and of EBITDA or Earnings Before Interest, Taxes, Depreciation and Amortization. By multiples we mean how many times greater is the TEV than the company's revenues or EBITDA, as the case may be?

Why do we care about 'TEV'? It tells us whether the price of the LBO is within our reach.

At this point revenue should be a fairly straightforward concept. It is the first line of the income statement, sometimes generically referred to as 'the top line' in casual conversation. You may, for example, hear a research analyst on television say, "We expect earnings to be good, but anticipate they will miss on the top line." Translation: based on our research, we expect the company to have positive net income, perhaps above expectations previously given by the company's management team, but we do not expect the company's revenues to meet those same expectations. A statement like this would imply some form of cost cutting is going on at the firm that would mathematically allow it to have lower revenues, but still realize higher net income.

A simplified net income equation explains that if our revenues are lower, but our net income is higher, we must have reduced our costs and/or taxes in order for such a scenario to be possible:

```
revenues - expenses - tax = net income
```

EBITDA is sometimes referred to as a proxy for cash flow. What this means is that EBITDA should provide a reasonable sense of the earnings generated by the operations of the firm. This is important because it provides a good indication of how well the company generates earnings for its owners.

For example, if you are the owner of a popular ice cream shop in town and at the end of the summer you take a look at your financial records to see how well you did – are you more interested in your earnings before or after expensing the depreciation on your soft serve machines? Of course, you are more concerned with the earnings before depreciation!

You may be wondering why this is. The reason for this is because, as the owner of the ice cream shop, you do not send money each month to ACME

Depreciation Co. as you do to your dairy suppliers and the utility company. Instead, the depreciation figure becomes important when it is time to consider tax because depreciation can affect taxable income – and this *is* something every shop owner is concerned with!

CHAPTER 6

INCOME STATEMENT

U p to this point we have identified the uses of funds for the transaction; the sources of funds that will be required to meet our uses; as well as the transaction enterprise value for our LBO. We have also discussed how to consider the potential value of the transaction relative to revenues and earnings before interest, taxes, depreciation and amortization or EBITDA.

With that said, now would be a good time for us to take a look at the income statement of our example company. The income statement can be found within the financial statements section of the annual report, which nowadays is available on most companies' web sites. In the United States there is also something known as a 10-K filing, which can be located on the Securities and Exchange Commission's EDGAR database and is a required filing of all publicly traded companies in the United States.

	A B C	D	E	F	G	H	I	J
29	ABC Company							
30	Income Statement							
31	(Dollars in millions)							
32					Pro Forma			
33			Year 0	Year 1	Year 2	Year 3	Year 4	Year 5
34	Net Revenue		$20,000	$21,400	$22,898	$24,501	$26,216	$28,051
35								
36	Expenses							
37	Cost of Goods Sold		12,300	13,161	14,082	15,068	16,123	17,251
38	Selling, General and Administrative		6,200	6,634	7,098	7,595	8,127	8,696
39	Other and Misc.		20	20	20	20	20	20
40	Total Expenses		18,520	19,815	21,201	22,683	24,270	25,967
41								
42	Operating Income		1,480	1,585	1,697	1,818	1,946	2,084
43	Interest Expense		-531	-531	-515	-495	-473	-447
44	Interest Income		13	13	13	13	13	13
45	Pre-Tax Income		961	1,066	1,195	1,335	1,486	1,649
46	Taxes		-336	-373	-418	-467	-520	-577
47	Net Income		$ 625	$ 693	$ 777	$ 868	$ 966	$ 1,072
48								
49	EBITDA		$ 1,880	$ 2,013	$ 2,155	$ 2,308	$ 2,471	$ 2,645
50	EBITDA Margin		9.4%	9.4%	9.4%	9.4%	9.4%	9.4%
51								
52	Revenue Growth Rate (Annual)			7.0%	7.0%	7.0%	7.0%	7.0%
53								
54	Depreciation and Amortization		$400	$428	$458	$490	$524	$561
55								
56	Percentage of Revenue							
57	Cost of Goods Sold		61.5%	61.5%	61.5%	61.5%	61.5%	61.5%
58	Selling, General and Administrative		31.0%	31.0%	31.0%	31.0%	31.0%	31.0%
59	Depreciation and Amortization		2.0%	2.0%	2.0%	2.0%	2.0%	2.0%
60								
61	Tax Rate		35.0%	35.0%	35.0%	35.0%	35.0%	35.0%

Income statement

If we look in the annual report of our company and locate the income statement we see that in the most recent fiscal year the company had the following revenue and expense breakdown:

- revenues, net: $20,000

- cost of goods sold: $12,300

- sales, general and administrative: $6,200

- other expenses: $20.

NET REVENUES

The **net revenues** figure is a reflection of how much money the company was able to generate through the selling of its products and merchandise after taking into consideration returned merchandise. The fact that these results are net of returns is important because absolute sales can be misleading when placing a valuation based on the financial performance of a company. For example, let's assume that you are part of a buyout group that is considering the purchase of a niche luxury home-decorating company. One of the major sales items for the company is expensive patio furniture and the company has a several-year track record of growing its patio furniture product sales. However, for the past two years all patio recliners and sofas have been experiencing an issue with the wheels falling off the legs of the furniture, which has resulted in 30% returns of all sales. Of those returns, half of the customers opt for a cash reimbursement and the other half exchange for a new version of the same product.

When we consider how well the company is performing at growing its sales figures, we would be deceived if we were to look at gross sales figures and not take into consideration the significant amount of returns that are taking place. This becomes even more important when attempting to place a valuation on the company as a multiple of its sales figures. We should be certain to look at the company's net sales figures to ensure that we are in fact considering the revenue that the company is generating and contributing towards its net income.

COST OF GOODS SOLD (COGS)

Cost of goods sold or COGS is an aggregation of all expenses that went into creating or procuring the product or merchandise sold. In our prior example of the luxury home-decorating company, let's consider the cost of goods sold associated with the patio furniture. The first costs that come to mind are raw materials. The patio furniture product is a combination of a metal rolling base, wood frame, and a stain-resistant microfiber. In addition to the raw materials, the direct labor that is associated with creating the product is also considered. By direct labor we are specifically referring to the work that is done at the company factory in crafting the product into a finished piece of furniture. Costs such as delivery and marketing of the finished product are not generally considered costs of goods sold and instead may appear in our next line item expense.

SALES, GENERAL AND ADMINISTRATIVE EXPENSE (SG&A)

Sales, general and administrative expense or SG&A is made up of items such as commissions paid to sales people, marketing of the product, and administrative expenses that go along with running the business. These are regular expenses that should be fairly predictable based on the volume of sales generated each period.

OTHER EXPENSES

Finally, **other expenses** are essentially everything else that does not fall under cost of goods sold or SG&A. These expenses are typically less correlated to sales volumes. An example of other expenses could include minor expenditures on renovating a showroom floor or purchasing new uniforms for staff. The point is these expenses should not be directly tied to the cost of producing the finished product nor directly tied to the selling of the product or the running of the business. These expenses should be non-recurring and miscellaneous in nature.

> 'Other expenses' should be non-recurring and miscellaneous – not tied to the cost of producing or selling products, or running the business.

Looking a bit closer at the income statement you may be asking why we did not address net interest expense with the other income statement line items. The reason for this is because we are going to calculate our own pro forma net interest expense that will be based on the capital structure being contemplated for this specific buyout transaction. For the purpose of focusing on the fundamentals of LBO analysis we will not consider bond premiums or unamortized costs; however, you may wish to do further research of your own to understand the treatment of these factors.

OPERATING INCOME

The total expense figure that we will focus on is the sum of COGS, SG&A and other expenses. In cell (E42) we will calculate the **operating income** by taking net revenues and subtracting the total expense figure, which we just calculated. This will give us an operating income of $1,480 million in Year 1. Operating income tells us a lot about a company's ability to generate earnings based on the pure costs and revenues associated with the product. You can think of this as the heart of the business – free from other considerations, such as the costs of financing and tax expense.

FUTURE GROWTH

Now that we have finished assembling the historical income statement information for our analysis we can turn our attention to the future growth of the company. Let's start with the top line. The **revenue growth** rates, which are assumptions, will be critical in several facets of our analysis because it is these assumptions that drive the overall growth and, as a matter of course, value of the company.

> Revenue growth rates will be critical – these assumptions underpin future growth and, therefore, the company's value.

In Year 1 of revenue growth, cell (F52), we use an **assumed growth rate** of 7.0%. How did we come to this assumed growth rate for the company? This is generally done by taking into consideration such things as historical growth rate trends for the company in question, general growth in the larger industry or economy, as well as other things that we may believe we know about the company. We are assuming that the company will grow sales at this same rate of 7.0% over the explicit forecast range of five years. For this reason, we will copy our Year 1 growth rate of 7.0% and paste it into the pro forma forecasts for years two (G52) through five (J52).

The keyboard shortcut for doing this can save a significant amount of time over the course of building your entire model. In order to use the keyboard shortcut in this instance you will need to highlight cells (G52) through (J52). Starting from cell (G52), while holding down the SHIFT key press the right arrow key until you arrive at cell (J52), or three times. Now that you have the desired cell range highlighted, enter the formula: =F52 and while holding down the CTRL button, press ENTER. You should now see your desired revenue growth rate of 7.0% across the explicit forecast range for years one through five.

CHAPTER 7
COST
STRUCTURE

EXPENSES

While future revenue growth is certainly one of the key considerations when creating a meaningful LBO analysis, there are several other items that must be taken into account to provide a complete financial view of the company under consideration. We have covered the topic of money coming in the door. Now we can consider the money that is going out the door. In other words, we now shift our focus to the topic of expenses.

There are two different types of expenses that we must differentiate between.

> We must differentiate between cash and non-cash expenses: raw materials and salaries on the one hand, and depreciation and amortization on the other.

- The first group of expenses is often called **cash expenses**. This type of expense is made up of items such as raw materials used to manufacture products, salaries paid to employees, bills paid to utility companies, etc. This type of expense should be fairly straightforward.

- The second type of expense is often referred to as **non-cash expenses**. A fairly common example of a non-cash expense often found on corporate financial statements is depreciation and amortization. There are a number of different methods to calculate depreciation. Some of the more well-known methods include: straight-line method, declining balance method, and sum of years' digits method. The distinguishing characteristics and methods of how to calculate each is beyond the scope of our analysis – the important thing to know is that depreciation is a means of allocating cost (net of any expected income from the future sale of the item) over the useful life of an asset.

In order to distinguish between cash and non-cash expenses for a given time period only one question must be asked: does the company need to pay out money at the end of the period for this expense? In the case of raw materials, salaries, and utility bills the answer it an emphatic yes! The company would not have workers very long if it did not make its payroll every month. Nor would suppliers or utility companies keep providing their product if cash payments were not received for their products.

> Distinguish between cash and non-cash expenses by asking: must the company pay out money for it at the end of a given period?

In the case of non-cash expenses, the answer is no, the company does not issue payments each month to make good on its monthly depreciation expense. However, depreciation expenses still appear on the income statement. This example should make the distinguishing of cash and non-cash expenses a bit easier to grasp.

Now that we have distinguished between the cash and non-cash expenses that appear on the income statement, let's bring in the non-cash expense of depreciation and amortization for Year 0 in our model. We will find the depreciation and amortization figure(s) broken out in the cash flow statement of the company's financials. In our example, we see that depreciation and amortization in the last full fiscal year was $400.

As you may have guessed, the $400 for depreciation and amortization is added back in the cash flow statement because depreciation and amortization are non-cash expenses; however, the expense is subtracted within the income statement. In order to get an accurate reflection of the company's cash-generating abilities in the previous period, we will add back the non-cash expenses to our EBITDA figure (E49). Let's hold off on calculated EBITDA for now, as we will return to this point later in the analysis.

REVEALING RATIOS

We are now in a good position to approximate the future expense structure for our example company. In order to do this, we need to calculate some ratios from the prior period.

COGS-TO-REVENUE RATIO

Looking at the **cost of goods sold as a percentage of revenue** for Year 0, cell (E57), we can determine the company's **COGS-to-revenue ratio** by dividing **cost of goods sold** for Year 0 (E37) by **net revenue** of Year 0 (E34). Calculating this figure gives us a COGS-to-revenue ratio of 61.5%.

This means that the company spends about 62 cents in product costs for every dollar of revenue that comes in. This figure does not include the costs associated with selling the item or the costs associated with running the business, such as salaries paid to bookkeepers, the cost of office supplies and non-product-related expenses.

SG&A-TO-REVENUE RATIO

Many of the non-product-related expenses are instead captured in the selling, general, and administrative (SG&A) expense line in the income statement. These costs are generally associated with the cost of running the business, separate from product costs. Just as we did for COGS, we will calculate a **SG&A-to-revenue ratio**, which will tell us what the company's SG&A expenses were for the prior period as a percentage of revenue.

To do this, we begin in cell (E58) and divide **SG&A expense** for Year 0 (E38) by **net revenue** of year 0 (E34). This results in an **SG&A-to-revenue ratio** of 31.0% for Year 0. This figure is telling us that in the prior period, it cost the company almost 31 cents in sales and office-related expenses per every dollar generated.

In order to optimize the use of your time, the formula for COGS-to-revenue in cell (E57) should look like the following: =E37/E$34. In cell (E58), given that we use the same type of ratio for SGA as in cell (E57), you can simply press CTRL+D. This will automatically take the formula for COGS-to-revenue (E57) and shift down one cell, changing the numerator to the SG&A figure for Year 0 (E38), while keeping the denominator of net revenue for Year 0 (E34) unchanged.

DEPRECIATION AND AMORTIZATION-TO-REVENUE RATIO

The final expense ratio we need to calculate in our example is that for **depreciation and amortization** (E59). We divide the depreciation and amortization (E54), which we took from the company's cash flow statement for the prior period, by the net revenue figure (E34). This results in a depreciation and amortization-to-revenue ratio of approximately 2%.

Similar to the ratios for COGS and SG&A, this ratio indicates that the company had depreciation and amortization charges of 2 cents for every dollar of revenue that was generated in the previous period. As the company grows and increases production, it stands to reason that it will be required to increase plant property and equipment to keep up with production demands. This will result in increased depreciation expenses associated with the increase in equipment. For the purposes of this book and in an effort to keep the focus on the fundamentals of LBO analysis we will use this simplified logic to forecast depreciation and amortization into the future.

> Depreciation and amortization-to-revenue is the final expense ratio we need to calculate.

IN THE YEARS AHEAD

At this time you should have percentage of revenue ratios for COGS (61.5%), SG&A (31.0%) and depreciation and amortization (2.0%) all for Year 0. We will use the same expense structure, which we calculated from the prior fiscal period, to make what we believe is a reasonable formulation of what the company's expense structure will look like in the explicit forecast period of years one through five.

In order to do this we begin at the **COGS-to-revenue ratio** for Year 1 (F57) and make that equal to the prior period's figure (E57) of 61.3%. We will then continue this by making the ratio of COGS-to-revenue for Year 2 equal to that of Year 1. This will be done through Year 5 for COGS and will be repeated for SG&A-to-revenue as well as for depreciation and amortization-to-revenue.

The process for getting our assumed expense ratios in place can be greatly sped up by using some keyboard shortcuts. In this case, we will again start in cell (F57). From cell (F57), highlight down and across to cell (J59) by holding down the shift button while using the arrow keys to navigate to the desired cells. Now we can enter our formula (with the cells remaining highlighted) just as we did in the original example above. The formula in cell (F57) should be the following: =E57. The key difference (along with the desired range being highlighted) is holding down CTRL while pressing ENTER (CTRL+ENTER). This will apply the same formula or logic that is entered into cell (F57) across the entire highlighted range in far fewer keystrokes.

Your expense ratios section should now look like the following:

◇	A	B	C	D	E	F	G	H	I	J
56	Percentage of Revenue									
57	Cost of Goods Sold				61.5%	61.5%	61.5%	61.5%	61.5%	61.5%
58	Selling, General and Administrtive				31.0%	31.0%	31.0%	31.0%	31.0%	31.0%
59	Depreciation and Amortization				2.0%	2.0%	2.0%	2.0%	2.0%	2.0%

Expense ratios

CHAPTER 8

INCOME STATEMENT FORECAST

Given our stated assumption that the percentage of revenue ratios for COGS, SG&A and depreciation and amortization for the explicit forecast range will be the same in years one through five as Year 0, we can now begin forecasting out our pro forma income statement.

Before we jump into our revenue projections, let's first take care of an important number that we will come back to later on, depreciation and amortization. In order to arrive at our estimated depreciation and amortization for future periods we multiply the associated period's **projected revenue figure** (F34) by our assumed **depreciation and amortization-to-revenue ratio** (E59), which in this example is 2%. Starting from cell (F54) the formula should be the following: =F34*F59. Upon pressing ENTER cell (F54) should be equal to zero, as we have yet to calculate the projections for net revenue.

You should not be overly concerned with the zero value in cell (F54) yet as this is merely the result of some prep work that is being done before we work through the full income statement projections. The pro forma estimates for depreciation and amortization will populate automatically once we bring in our forecasted revenue figures. For now, let's finish our work for pro forma depreciation and amortization by applying the same formula used in Year 1, net revenue x depreciation and amortization-to-revenue ratio, in years two through five. This can be done by starting in cell (G54) and multiplying the **forecasted net revenue figure** for Year 2 by the **depreciation and amortization-to-revenue ratio** in the same year and repeating the same formula for the following years. You can also use a keyboard shortcut.

The keyboard shortcut begins by starting in cell (F54). From (F54) hold down the SHIFT key while using the arrow keys to expand the highlighted area across to cell (J54). Once cells (F54) to (J54) are highlighted press CTRL+R. This keyboard shortcut copies the formula located in the far-left highlighted cell, in this case cell (F54), and applies that formula to the highlighted cells to the right (cells G54 through J54). In this case, cell (F54) is equal to the product of

Year 1 **pro forma revenue** and the Year 1 **depreciation and amortization-to-revenue ratio**. By highlighting (F54) through (J54) and pressing CTRL+R we mitigate the risk of entering a formula incorrectly in any of the following pro forma years; however, we must be certain that the original formula is correct, otherwise we will be using an incorrect formula throughout the explicit forecast range. Similar to the CTRL+D keyboard shortcut, CTRL+R can potentially save you a considerable amount of time over the course of creating complex financial analysis. When using any keyboard shortcut you must be aware of the inherent risks (e.g. copying errors) that go along with the benefits (e.g. time savings) of the shortcut.

We have set the table for building out the pro forma income statement forecast by laying out assumptions regarding annual revenue growth and the relative cost structure of the company over the explicit forecast range of five years.

Note that we did not change the relative cost structure of the firm from the current state; instead, we assumed that relative costs-to-revenue would remain unchanged over the next five-year period. In the case that we knew something in the future was going to affect one of the relative costs (either increase or decrease the relative cost-to-revenue ratio), at some point in the explicit forecast range and continue to do so into the future, we would adjust the affected ratio within the fiscal year of the change and continue to use the new cost-to-revenue ratio in the following years. (This assumes that the change in costs structure is of a more permanent nature and not a one-off occurrence that is the result of extraordinary circumstances for a brief period of time.)

> We have assumed that relative costs-to-revenue will remain unchanged over the next five years. If we know this won't be the case, we adjust the affected ratio.

FORECASTING YEAR 1

All the pieces are in place to forecast out our income statement. The only thing left now is to do it. We start by focusing our attention on revenue for pro forma

Year 1 (F34). We are assuming that revenue will grow at a rate of 7.0% per annum. In other words, net revenue in Year 1 should be equal to the prior period's (Year 0) net revenue figure plus an additional 7.0%. In order to build a formula that does this correctly in our spreadsheet we start in cell (F34) and enter the following formula: =E34*(1+F52). Notice that we are simply making the revenue of Year 1 equal to that of Year 0 and multiplying by 1 + the assumed revenue growth rate of the respective year.

At this point, you could continue to fill out the remainder of the pro forma years for net revenue in Row 34, but in the spirit of best practice we will instead focus on working down the line items of the income statement. You will eventually see why we choose to go about creating our analysis in this way. For now, it is only important to know that this method should save time over the course of building the LBO analysis.

Focusing on the COGS and SG&A section of the income statement, we have already spent a considerable amount of time explaining cost structure and the logic that goes behind the respective cost-to-revenue ratios that have been assumed for the explicit forecast range. We can now use these assumed percentage of revenue ratios to forecast out COGS and SG&A expenses in Year 1. Since we already know our forecasted net revenue figure for Year 1, we know that Year 1 COGS and SG&A will be 61.5% and 31.0%, respectively, of net revenue.

In order to reflect this in our LBO analysis we begin in cell (F37) and make Year 1 COGS expense equal to Year 1 net revenue multiplied by the forecasted COGS-to-revenue ratio of Year 1. The formula used in cell (F37) should look like the following: =F34*F57. Similarly for SG&A you will make Year 1 SG&A equal to Year 1 net revenue multiplied by the forecasted SG&A-to-revenue ratio for Year 1. Your SG&A expense ratio should be entered in cell (F38) and should be expressed as the following: =F34*F58.

You may wish to use a keyboard shortcut in this situation. Given that we are using a common input (net revenue in cell F34) and that we have cleverly set up our percentage of revenue ratios for COGS and SG&A in the same order as they appear in the income statement, we can save valuable time and a few key strokes by taking a different approach to setting up our formulas from the very beginning. Starting from Year 1 COGS (F37), rather than jumping directly into entering the formula into the cell, we begin by pressing the SHIFT key and arrow down key to highlight both Year 1 COGS and SG&A, cells (F37) to (F38), respectively. After this we will enter our formula the same as we did in the prior explanation for COGS expense, but with one exception. This time we will enter the formula with an anchored row for the net revenue input, which is represented by the dollar symbol, $. This will allow the formula that we use for Year 1 COGS to be carried down one row to Year 1 SG&A expense while maintaining the same revenue input (F34), but adjusting down one row to take in the SG&A percentage of revenue input for SG&A expense. All other aspect of the formula will remain the same. Your shortcut formula should look like the following: =F$34*F57. After entering this altered version of the formula press CTRL+ENTER. This will ensure that the formula is applied across all of the highlighted section. You have now successfully cut the number of required formula inputs in half!

This brings us to the line item of **other expenses**. For the purpose of this analysis we will assume that other expenses remain constant throughout the explicit forecast period. This should be considered a reasonable assumption, as this expense item is not a core expense that is inextricably tied to the scale of business. Rather, this expense line item is made up of non-core expenses that should not fluctuate a great deal with any change in the size of the business. This is the simplest type of formula we will use in our LBO analysis. We will simply set our Year 1 other expenses equal to that of Year 0 other expenses. Starting from cell (F39), enter the equation for Year 1 other expenses as the following: =E39.

> For the purpose of this analysis we will assume that other expenses remain constant throughout the explicit forecast period.

Now let's calculate the **total expenses** by summing our COGS, SG&A and other expenses for Year 1. This can be done by entering the following equation: =SUM(F37:F39). As an alternative to writing out the entire equation for Year 1 total expenses you may simply wish to press CTRL+R from the Year 1 total expenses cell. This will apply the formula from Year 0 total expenses to Year 1 total expenses. This is an acceptable alternative only because we are using the exact same formula to calculate total expenses in Year 1 as we did in Year 0.

We have reached a milestone in our LBO analysis. We are now able to calculate **operating income** for our first pro forma year in the explicit forecast range. Since we already have calculated operating income in the historic Year 0 financials (`operating income = net revenue - total operating expenses`), we can use this same formula and apply it to our just completed Year 1 operating items. Rather than writing in the formula manually, let's try using the keyboard shortcut, `CTRL+R`, to bring the Year 0 operating income formula over to the right by one cell. Doing this will complete the operating income section in our Year 1 pro forma income statement.

EXTENDING OUR PROJECTIONS

Given that we have completed Year 1's pro forma operating income we should be feeling fairly good about the work that has been done to this point. We only have four more pro forma years left before we complete the explicitly forecasted operating income section of our LBO analysis.

However, before we move on we have one last item to cover. The format and arrangement by which we originally set up our analysis was not by accident. Ideally, when setting up your leveraged buyout analysis (or any financial analysis), the format of your analysis should be arranged so that you are able to apply logic and formulas across any following pro forma projections as you desire, eliminating the need to duplicate your efforts in any following years of the explicit forecast range. Since we have taken care to ensure that we can apply our logic and formulas across all of the projected years in the explicit forecast range, we can complete all five years of net revenue, operating expense items, and operating income projections in a few key strokes. This can be done by copying the formulas we already put in place for pro forma Year 1 and pasting them in years two through five. This can either be done for each individual cell in the operating section of the income statement or a keyboard shortcut can be used.

Using the keyboard shortcut to this step begins with selecting or highlighting the entire operating section of the income statement. We start from Year 1 net revenue in cell (F34). While holding the SHIFT key, use the arrow keys to navigate down and to the right until reaching the final pro forma year of projected operating income (J42). At this point the entire operating section of the income statement should be highlighted. You are now ready to bring the formulas from pro forma Year 1 into pro forma Years 2-5. Press CTRL+R and all five years of pro forma operating projections should now be completed. Of course, these projections are based on our earlier assumptions and changing any of the assumptions that were laid out earlier should duly affect the projections that you see before you and ultimately affect the valuation of the company under consideration (to some degree) in our leveraged buyout analysis.

CHECKPOINT: ARE WE RIGHT?

At this point in time we have completed a fair amount of work in the process of creating our leveraged buyout analysis. We have brought in historical financial information of the potential buyout target, ABC Company, and calculated some essential operating ratios, all of which plays a key role in shaping the pro forma financial projections. We have made some assumptions regarding the future growth rate and cost structure of the company over the explicit forecast range. We have also forecasted and calculated operating income in the explicit forecast range for the target company. Considering that we have come this far it may not be a bad idea for us to check our work at this point.

> We've now completed a fair amount of work in the LBO analysis, which makes it a good time to check our work so far.

There is no one correct way to check the work of your leveraged buyout analysis, as long as it proves effective. One method you may consider for auditing the operating section of the income statement is spot-checking the formulas you have copied over from pro forma Year 1 by working through the line items of the final pro forma year, in this case, pro forma Year 5. Perhaps the most effective way to do this is by simply working backwards. Begin with the final calculation, in this case, operating income for the pro forma Year 5 (J42). Once your active cell is pro forma Year 5 operating income press the F2 key. This will place the active cell in formula editor mode and will make it easier to view the source input that makes up your formula for Year 5 operating income. Upon opening formula editor mode in pro forma Year 5 operating income you should see that the formula we have in place is correct. We are starting with the net revenues for the pro forma Year 5 and subtracting out the pro forma Year 5 operating expenses as we intended. This may seem like a time-consuming process, but with practice you will become very efficient in checking the source inputs of your formulas using the F2 key.

Before moving on, there is one other powerful check we will demonstrate. There is nothing worse in the process of building a leveraged buyout analysis than coming to the end of your financial model only to realize that a critical error has been made and then having to spend valuable time searching for the source of the error. To ensure that your time is not wasted, it is a good idea to periodically check your work and save different versions of your financial model (preferably in different locations) along the way. This next check will help ensure that your formulas are working as you intended and provides a quick means of auditing formulas of varying complexity.

A good way to check formulas are working as you intended is to substitute an input variable with the number one for multiplication and as the denominator for dividing within formulas. Likewise, the same is true for substituting a zero for added or subtracted input variables. This is particularly useful when dealing with complex formulas, when the result of the change in input variables is not so easily apparent.

> Substituting input variables with '1' is a good way to quickly check formulas.

Our simple example of this check put into practice begins with the pro forma Year 5 net revenue (J34). Open up the formula editor by pressing F2. Once in the formula editor, substitute the net revenue annual growth rate input variable (J52) with the number 0 (zero). (Note that this is a multiplication formula, but because the input variable is already being added to the number 1 we will substitute in a zero.) We are now multiplying the remaining input variable (pro forma Year 4 net revenue) by 1. Upon pressing ENTER we see that the result is, as expected, a number identical to that of pro forma Year 4 net revenue. This should not be a surprise as the formula we began with was a simple formula; however, in more complex formulas the answer may not be so easily recognizable and using a check similar to the previous example may prove an invaluable tool in auditing calculation in your analysis. Based on the result we know that our formula is working correctly and we can move onto the next course of business.

CHAPTER 9
INTEREST

SETTING THE STAGE

L ooking down our income statement, we can see that the next section is interest income and interest expense. This section is central to the leveraged buyout analysis, but before we are able to project these figures we must first know more information regarding the leverage or debt to be used in the contemplated transaction. We will be able to forecast interest income and interest expense projections once we have done some work on the cash and debt balances we expect to be carrying over the explicit forecast range. For now, we can simply set up the interest portion of the income statement by entering the formulas that will eventually provide us with pre-tax income. To do this, we begin in pre-tax income for the historical period Year 0 (E45). In order to calculate pre-tax income in our example we will need to net all of the following: operating income, interest income, and interest expense. Notice in our example that interest expense is a negative number. From cell E45 your formula should look like the following: =sum(E42:E44). This formula will give you the pre-tax income for Year 0.

We are able to use the SUM function in this case to calculate pre-tax income because interest expense is already a negative figure, so the addition of this negative figure has the same effect as subtracting

> Income and interest expense is central to the LBO analysis. We can forecast this section when we know the expected cash and debt balances going forward.

expense represented as a positive number. In general, it is easier to quickly calculate through a financial model if line items that should ultimately be subtracted from revenue (such as expenses) are represented as negative numbers in the historical and pro forma financial statements.

During the course of constructing your leverage buyout analysis or any corporate finance model you will undoubtedly need to calculate the sums of sub-sections in financial statements, just as we did for total expenses in the income statement. The pre-tax income section of our example income statement presents us with an opportunity to demonstrate another keyboard shortcut that will without doubt save you a great deal of time over the course of building your leveraged buyout analysis.

As we mentioned earlier, the formula for calculating pre-tax income from our example income statement is: `pre-tax income = operating income + interest income - interest expense`

As a formula in your spreadsheet, we said the formula should look like the following: `=sum(E42:E44)`. There are a number of different ways this formula could have been entered into your spreadsheet. You could have entered the formula in directly as notation taken from this book. You may have begun by pressing the equals sign and then typed in the SUM function followed by using the arrow keys to select the cells you desired to sum; you may even, Heaven forbid, have used the mouse at some point in the cell-selection process to reach the end formula: `=sum(E42:E44)`. All of these options would get you to the desired end goal of having the correct formula in place to calculate pre-tax income. However, the keyboard shortcut that gives you the desired formula in the shortest amount of time would have been (starting from pre-tax income for Year 0, cell (E45)): ALT+EQUALS. This keyboard shortcut would give you the formula: `=sum(E42:E44)` in one combined key stroke.

This keyboard shortcut works in this case because the ALT+EQUALS shortcut automatically sums the contiguous cells that are directly above the cell that the formula is being entered into. This also means that the shortcut would not give us the desired equation if there were an empty row in between **interest income** and **operating income**, as we have between **total expense** and **operating income**. It pays to think ahead when constructing the format or layout of your leveraged buyout model's financial statements because it will affect the way that you are able to use some of the keyboard shortcuts you learn in this book during the creation of your analysis. Of course, in order for this shortcut to be of any use to us we must also remember to represent expenses as negative numbers. Otherwise, in this case, we would have been adding interest expense to revenue, which would certainly have affected valuations in the end. There are many factors to consider when constructing the financial statements for analysis and using keyboard shortcuts, but over time these factors will become second nature as you develop your own style and favored shortcuts when constructing financial analysis.

TAXES

It is said that the only two certainties in this life are death and taxes. Unfortunately, LBOs do not escape the latter.

For the purposes of our example, we will assume a corporate tax rate of 35%. In the case of historical Year 0, we are entering 35% directly into cell (E61), but it should be noted that this is a simplification that is done only to allow us to instead focus on the fundamentals of building the LBO analysis. In practice, when dealing with historical financials, tax expense for the period will be explicitly outlined in the annual or quarterly financial statements. Based on the disclosure in the financial statements we can calculate the effective tax rate paid by the company by dividing the tax expense by pre-tax income:

```
effective tax rate = tax expense / pre-tax income
```

Determining the effective tax rate for a company over the past couple of years should provide a reasonable basis for making some assumptions about the tax rate the company is likely to be subject to in the near future (i.e. the explicit forecast range). However, this book is not dedicated to the subject of tax brackets, loopholes, or any other tax specialty and for that reason we will continue with the default US tax rate of 35%.

Now that we have brought in the tax rate of 35% for Year 0 we must also bring in the assumed tax rate for the target company in the pro forma years one through five. We will assume the same tax rate of 35% will apply in the explicit forecast range, as we have no reason to believe the tax rate will change for the company over the following five-year period. To do this we will set the values of pro forma tax rate assumptions in years one through five of our income statement equal to the historic Year 1 value or 35%.

Since we already have the value that we want to use in years one through five in Year 0 we can easily bring this number (the assumed corporate tax rate) across our explicit forecast range in only a few key strokes. We start off by moving to the Year 1 **tax rate projection** cell (F61). From here we highlight across to the Year 5 **tax rate projection** cell (J61) by holding the SHIFT key while using the arrow keys to navigate across. Enter the formula =E61 (while cells remain highlighted) and press CTRL+ENTER. Each of the highlighted cells now references the cell that is immediately to the left of itself. If we change the original cell (E61) all of five pro forma tax rates assumptions for years one through five in our explicit forecast range will change to that same number.

Although we have yet to bring **interest income** and **interest expense** into our pro forma analysis we must still continue to prepare the income statement to calculate our projections correctly once we get to that point. For that reason we will continue down the path of preparation, putting in place our formulas for calculating **tax expense** based on our newly formed tax rate assumptions for Year 1 through Year 5. We start by calculating the tax expense for Year 0. Tax expense is calculated based on the historical financial information we pulled from the target company's annual filings that lead to the current year's pre-tax income and our assumed corporate tax rate of 35%. The formula for calculating tax expense is:

```
tax expense = pre-tax income x corporate tax rate
```

In cell (E46) this equation is represented as the following: =-E45*E61. Tax expense is, after all, subtracted from pre-tax income and for that reason we enter this formula with a negative sign before cell (E45). This ensures that the product of this equation appears as a negative number in Year 0 of our income statement. This will also allow the easy use of the SUM function later on when we calculate net income.

We have now arrived at the bottom line: net income.

Now we have arrived at the bottom line, **net income**. You can go ahead and calculate net income using the SUM function we just talked about. We will be summing a positive pre-tax income number and a negative tax expense number. The SUM function will give us the net figure of these two numbers. Just as we demonstrated before, beginning in cell (E47), we enter the formula: sum(E45:E46). The keyboard shortcut ALT+EQUALS is not a perfect fit for this scenario, but you can still make it work by pressing ALT+EQUALS from cell (E47) and then holding the SHIFT key and pressing the up arrow key once, followed by ENTER. This will result in the correct formula to calculate net income in our pro forma income statement for Year 0.

CHAPTER 10
EBITDA

Earnings Before Interest, Taxes, and Depreciation and Amortization is a mouthful. The finance community has naturally enough, therefore, grown accustomed to using the acronym EBITDA. To calculate EBITDA you start with net income and simply add back any interest, taxes, and depreciation and amortization expenses.

It's worth noting that EBITDA will not appear in any accountant review of a company. This is because EBITDA is not an accounting metric. Rather, it is a means of measuring a company's profitability. What is, perhaps, most significant about EBITDA is that it enables the comparison of profitability between companies *regardless* of capital structure and accounting treatment.

We can calculate EBITDA by first turning our attention to Year 0, cell (E49). As mentioned, EBITDA can be calculated a number of ways. It is essentially,

```
net  income  +  net  interest  expense  +  tax  expense  +
depreciation and amortization expense
```

Remember that in our example we represent expenses as negative numbers. For that reason, we will need to subtract the negative expense numbers to arrive at EBITDA. We begin in cell (E49) and set our formula to equal

```
net income (E47) - (negative) tax expense (E46) - (negative)
interest expense - interest income - (negative) depreciation
and amortization expense
```

This may seem counterintuitive at first, but developing a method to easily distinguish between positive income flows versus negative expense flows will help you and the beneficiaries of your analysis keep matters straight when reviewing financial analysis. However, formatting is a matter of subjective taste and you are encouraged to adhere to the taste of the person paying your salary!

Another way that you could have calculated EBITDA based on our example is to set the EBITDA (E49) formula equal to operating income (E42) plus depreciation and amortization expense (E54). This formula would work in our example because only net interest expense and tax expense stand between net income and operating income. This method would have saved you a few key strokes in the process of creating your EBITDA formula, but for the purposes of this book we chose to use the more detailed formula. Either formula will bring you to the correct figure on our example.

As we mentioned, EBITDA is a powerful tool for measuring profitability across different companies, while taking out considerations such as the amount and cost of debt on the balance sheet as well as tax treatment. The first cousin of EBITDA, in the family of financial metrics, is *EBITDA margin*. Like EBITDA, EBITDA margin is also an effective tool in measuring the profitability of a company. However, EBITDA margin is unique to EBITDA in that it is not concerned with the absolute size of business operations; instead it measures how adequate a company is at generating earnings (before interest, taxes, depreciation and amortization) relative to every dollar of revenue that is brought in. It is a good indicator of efficiency and a company's ability to drive profits from its revenues.

> EBITDA is a powerful tool for measuring profitability across different companies.

Calculating both EBITDA and EBITDA margin together provides a more complete analysis when comparing companies. While every company would like to have a relatively large EBITDA margin to report at the end of each fiscal year, it means very little if net revenues were down 90% from the previous year. Likewise, a relatively large EBITDA figure is always more desirable than a small one, but few executives would be bragging if EBITDA for the year end increased by $1 million while net revenues for the year increased by $100 million. The operating efficiency of the company, in this hypothetical case, went down the tubes. While EBITDA may have increased by $1 million for the year, the executive would most likely be looking for another job in the near future because of the poor operating efficiency of the company, as measured by the decline in EBITDA margin. In summary, both EBITDA and EBITDA margin are potent measures of profitability that level the playing field regarding capital structure and tax treatment. However, they should be calculated together in order to provide a more complete picture of a company's profitability on both an absolute and relative basis.

Up to this point, you have completed the entire Year 0 column in the income statement for all the items that we are able to address at this time. The only line items that should still remain unaddressed in Year 0 of your income statement are interest income and interest expense. Since we have completed all other aspects of the income statement and because we are not ready to address net interest expense yet, we can now complete years one through five in the explicit forecast range of your income statement. You can do this the same way you filled out the remaining years of the operating section of the income statement a few steps back. Congratulations on completing over 90% of the income statement.

Try using the keyboard shortcut that we demonstrated earlier by starting in cell (E45) and using the SHIFT key and ARROW keys to highlight the area from (E45) through (J50). This covers the area from pre tax income in Year 0 to EBITDA margin in pro forma Year 5. Once this area is highlighted, press CTRL+R. The remainder of your income statement for the pro forma years one through five should fully populate and transfer each row's corresponding formulas accordingly.

CHAPTER 11

CASH FLOW

s you will see in this section, cash flow will dictate the target company's ability to pay down the debt of the contemplated leveraged buyout capital structure and ultimately drive returns for the potential buyers of the company. We will start our cash flow analysis with net income and add back non-cash charges from the income statement. In our example we will also make some simple assumptions about the operating requirements of the company as they relate to net working capital as well as capital expenditure requirements. These assumptions are made so that rather than get entangled in the details of basic corporate finance we can move quickly to focus on the unique aspects of leveraged buyout analysis.

> Cash flow dictates a target company's ability to pay down debt – and ultimately drive returns for the investor.

	L	M	N	O	P	Q	R	S	T	U
29	ABC Company									
30	Cash Flow and Debt Sweep Analysis									
31	(Dollars in millions)									
32							Pro Forma			
33					Year 0	Year 1	Year 2	Year 3	Year 4	Year 5
34	Net Income					$ 693	$ 777	$ 868	$ 966	$ 1,072
35	Depreciation					428	458	490	524	561
36	Capital Expenditures					(428)	(458)	(490)	(524)	(561)
37	Change in Net Working Capital (1.5% Rev)				1.5%	(321)	(343)	(368)	(393)	(421)
38	Cash Flow for Debt Repayments					$ 372	$ 433	$ 500	$ 573	$ 651
39										
40	Debt Balance									
41	Beginning Balance	Rate	4.5%		$ 11,810	$ 11,438	$ 11,005	$ 10,505	$ 9,932	
42	Borrowing / (Paydown)					(372)	(433)	(500)	(573)	(651)
43	Ending Balance			$ 11,810	$ 11,438	$ 11,005	$ 10,505	$ 9,932	$ 9,281	
44										
45	Cash Balance									
46	Beginning Balance	Rate	2.5%		$ 500	$ 500	$ 500	$ 500	$ 500	
47	Additions					-	-	-	-	-
48	Ending Balance			$ 500	$ 500	$ 500	$ 500	$ 500	$ 500	

Cash flow and debt sweep analysis

Begin your simplified (but sufficient) cash flow by bringing in net income information from your income statement directly into the cash flow section for pro forma Year 1. As you may have expected, we are not interested in Year 0 at this time. In order to transfer the pro forma Year 1 net income result into your cash flow, be sure to reference the income statement directly by using the following formula in cell (Q34): =F47. Do not copy and paste the formula into the Year 1 cash flow section of your analysis, as this will result in an incorrect figure. By referencing the net income cell for pro forma Year 1 in the income statement your cash flow will automatically adjust to any changes in our net income projections going forward.

As we covered earlier, depreciation is a non-cash expense. In other words, depreciation is deducted from net revenues on the income statement, but no one at the company ever makes out a payment for the depreciation or amortization expense the company incurred for the period. As that is the case, we need to add back depreciation and amortization expense to net income as part of deriving cash flow for the period.

In our example, we represent expenses as negative items because they are being subtracted from net revenue.

In your simple cash flow section, add back the depreciation and amortization expense that is listed in the income statement. Make sure that you are aware of which items are represented as negative numbers and which items are represented as positive numbers, as this will affect the way you add items back.

In our example, we are representing expenses as negative items because they are being subtracted from net revenue. For this reason, we add depreciation and amortization back to net income by using a negative before the referenced depreciation figure. Just as we did for net income, be sure that you reference the depreciation and amortization expense directly from the income statement (while using a negative sign). This will allow your cash flow to automatically update with any changes that occur within the income statement. Your formula for adding back depreciation and amortization within our cash flow section (Q35) should look like the following: =-F54.

Looking down our cash flow analysis we next have to consider any capital expenditures we believe the target company is going to make over the course of the explicit forecast range. In this example, let's assume that we believe the target company is going to make capital expenditure equal to the depreciation of the equipment is currently has. To represent this, begin by setting cell (Q36) as =-Q35. Apply this formula across the rest of the row and be sure to keep the negative sign in front of your equation. Doing this effectively says that the company will invest in new equipment at a relatively steady rate that mirrors the depreciation of existing assets.

The final item for consideration in the cash flow analysis is change in net working capital. Net working capital is defined as current assets less current liabilities and can be thought of as a measure of a company's short term financial health.

```
net working capital = current assets - current liabilities
```

As a business grows, the requirements for working capital typically expand with the growth of the business. We assume that the target company in our example is no exception. For that reason, we assume that the change in net working capital will be 1.5% of net revenue. This simple assumption follows the fundamental understanding that net working capital requirements will grow with the expansion of the business, but it bears mentioning that in practice you may wish for a breakdown of each item that makes up net working capital and do an individual forecast for each based on the believed requirements of the company over the forecast period. For our example and for the purposes of staying within the scope of this book, we will make a safe and conservative assumption that net working capital requirements grow in line with the business as 1.5% of net revenues.

> As a business grows, the requirements for working capital typically expand.

In order to reflect the pro forma projection for changes in net working capital correctly within the cash flow analysis portion of your model, begin in Year 1 (Q37) and multiply net revenue (taken from the income statement) by our assumed 1.5%, which we explained in great detail above. It is important to note that because the requirement for net working capital is increasing it means that cash will be spent to meet this requirement. For this reason, it is important to ensure that increases in net working capital are reflected as cash outflows (negative) and decreases in net working capital are reflected as cash inflows. In our example, we will use a negative sign before the 1.5% in cell (P37). In addition to this, because the 1.5% of net revenue assumption for change in net working capital will apply across all five years in the explicit forecast range, as a matter of good practice, we anchor the column when referencing the 1.5% net working capital assumption. At this point in time your formula should look like the following in cell (Q37): =F49*-$P37.

Anchoring is a command that, in the context of financial modeling, tells the spreadsheet not to change the anchored reference cell when the formula is copied and applied in different cells. During the course of constructing this leveraged buyout analysis or any other financial analysis dealing with assumptions across multiple pro forma years you will most likely want to use anchoring in your formulas so that your formulas can be applied across different rows or columns in just a few key strokes. (The alternative is re-entering the formula a separate time for each individual cell.)

A dollar sign is used in Microsoft Excel to represent anchoring. A dollar sign in front of the first portion of a cell reference name (the letter) means, 'Do not change the referenced column for this input in the case of applying the formula in different cells'. (Example: $A1)

We used this kind of anchoring in our formula for projecting changes in net working capital. In that example we anchored column P with a dollar sign because we want to eventually apply the 1.5% portion of the formula to the following pro forma net revenues in Years 2 –5, which are placed in the following columns. So how do we go about applying anchoring to our formulas? The most obvious way is by simply entering a dollar sign at the point of entering the formula.

This is a fine way if you know where you will need anchoring at every turn in your model. However, it may become tiresome any time you realize after the formula has already been entered that anchoring should have been used with one of the input variables and you then have to enter the formula editor, move to the column or row section of the cell reference name and then press SHIFT+4 to get your anchoring dollar sign in place. A quicker way to get your reference cell anchoring in place is to use the F4 key. You will still need to be in formula editor and navigate to the cell you wish to anchor. Once your cursor is touching any part of the cell reference name (e.g. A1) hit the F4 key and dollar signs will appear in front of both the row and column indicators of the reference name. That cell is now being instructed to change neither row nor column in the event the formula is copied and pasted in another cell. Hit F4 one more time and the dollar sign only appears in front of the row indicator. Hit the F4 key a third time and the anchor is applied only to the column, allowing the reference row to move up and down with the copying and pasting of the formula in different cells. Finally a fourth stroke on F4 will remove all anchoring. The F4 key is a quick way to toggle through anchoring in the formula editor. You may wish to consider using it if you notice yourself doing a fair amount of anchoring in your financial modeling.

Some common examples of this are accounts payable and accounts receivable. When a company pays down its accounts payable (a current liability) it is, obviously, a cash outflow. Conversely, if accounts payable continue to increase without being paid down it is considered a cash inflow because we are able to buy such things as inventory with having to decrease the company's cash balance. The same holds true for accounts receivable (a current asset). If accounts receivable is reduced, it is a cash inflow to the company. However, if accounts receivable is not reduced, but rather it increases as inventory continues to leave the store on credit – that would most certainly be considered a cash outflow.

Now that we have estimated all the components of pro forma Year 1 cash flow available for debt repayments we can sum these line items to project the amount of debt the target company will likely be able to pay down in pro forma Year 1 based on our assumptions. (Try using the ALT+EQUALS keyboard shortcut in this case to get your answer.)

In summing the Year 1 pro forma cash flow available for debt repayment components we calculate a figure of $372 million. This is the amount of cash generated by the business that, after cash expenditures required to grow and operate the business, could be used to pay down the debt that would be used by our buyout group to purchase the target company. This is an important figure in the leveraged buyout analysis because as a potential buyer of the target company it is important to know to what degree the target company

> Summing Year 1 pro forma cash flow available for debt repayment gives us the figure that could be used to pay down the debt incurred in buying the company.

would be able to pay down the proposed debt that would be used to purchase the company. Larger debt balances generally mean larger interest expense.

Potential bidders for the target company would want to avoid entering into a transaction where they end up being the owners of a company that is drowning in its own interest expense and unable to pay down its debts. For that reason, the sooner the target company is expected to be able to pay down debt, the more attractive the leveraged buyout may appear to potential buyers.

CHAPTER 12

OUTSTANDING DEBT BALANCE

Thus far we have covered the pro forma profitability (before net interest consideration) of the target company in our contemplated leveraged buyout analysis, as well as the projected cash flow available for debt repayment generated by the business in Year 1 of the explicit forecast range. As we did in our income statement, we will leave remaining years of the pro forma forecast range until the end, once we finish Year 1 and ensure that our formulas are correct and ready to be expanded to the following years. We are on our way to determining what the cost of financing the leveraged buyout will be in the form of net interest expense. The next step in the process of making that determination is projecting the debt balances on which interest expense is charged.

In the first portion of our leveraged buyout model we performed a 'uses and sources of funds' analysis. There we determined the amount of money required to purchase the target company's equity, refinance the existing debt, and cover the cost of transaction fees. It is worth repeating that, in our example, we assume that we are refinancing the debt that currently exists on the company's balance sheet. For that reason, the assumed pro forma debt balance will carry one uniform interest rate charged on the new projected debt balance. The old debt balance will effectively cease to exist, as we are assuming that it is paid down through the refinancing.

> At this stage, we are on our way to determining the cost of financing the LBO in the form of net interest expense.

Looking at the proposed sources of funds, we see that we assume to pay for the cost of the proposed transaction with $4,500 million of equity financing and $11,810 million of debt financing. The assumed debt financing of $11,810 million will be the new pro forma debt balance at the end of Year 0 in our debt sweep analysis and is the amount on which interest expense will be calculated in the pro forma years.

Bring the assumed debt financing from our sources and uses of cash analysis into Year 0 of the debt sweep (P43) by referencing the debt financing amount as a direct cell formula reference. Your formula in cell (P43) should look like the following: =F13. (Try using the keyboard shortcut F4 to anchor both the row and the column of your reference cell just to get in the practice of using anchoring.)

Another way to think of the Year 0 ending debt balance is as the Year 1 beginning debt balance. After all, this is the starting point from which interest expense is going to be charged in Year 1. For that reason, we will take our Year 0 ending debt balance and use it as our beginning outstanding debt balance in pro forma Year 1.

To do this, we begin in pro forma Year 1 of our outstanding debt analysis (Q41) and directly reference the Year 0 outstanding debt ending balance (P43). Your formula in cell (Q41) should look like the following: =P43. (Note that we do not use any anchoring in this formula.)

PAYING DOWN LEVERAGE – HOW MUCH IS THE RIGHT AMOUNT?

Perhaps the most important question in the financial analysis of leveraged buyouts is – To what degree can or should debt be paid down after the closing of a leveraged buyout transaction? This is a significant issue because the paying down of debt will have a direct impact on the interest expense of the company, which will positively affect the profitability and cash flow of the company. Put another way, the faster the owners of the business can pay down the debt, the sooner they will have a greater share of the profits for themselves.

The question of how much debt should be paid down in a period is determined by a couple of factors. The first factor is a matter of cash flow. In the previous section we calculated the cash flow that would be available for debt repayments in pro forma Year 1. This figure is a function of net income plus our non-cash expense of depreciation, less any required capital expenditures, which we said would take place every two years, less any changes in net working capital. The result of this calculation will provide us with the dollar amount of debt that the target company is projected to have available from its pro forma cash flow. The second consideration when determining the amount of debt to pay down in a period is the actual amount of debt that is outstanding at the time of payment. If cash flow is available to pay down debt greater than the amount of debt currently outstanding, you would be well served to make a payment only for the amount of debt you actually owe. In other words, your debt repayment at the end of the period should be the smaller balance between 1) the cash flow available for debt repayment and 2) the balance of current outstanding debt.

> The question of how much debt should be paid down is determined by cash flow and debt outstanding at the time.

Now the question is – How do we represent the logic of paying the smaller amount of cash available for debt paydown versus the current amount of total debt outstanding? The answer is the MIN function. The MIN function in Microsoft Excel chooses the smallest value among selected cells. In our example, we are making the comparison between cash flow available for repayment (Q38) and the beginning debt balance (Q41). It must be highlighted that in the event the target company is not profitable and instead has a negative value for cash flow available for debt repayment, the company would need to borrow additional debt in order to meet its financial obligations. This factor will also be incorporated into our formula.

The debt paydown or additional borrowing formula begins in pro forma Year 1 of our outstanding debt balance analysis (Q42). Debt paydowns will be represented as negative numbers, as these payments would reduce the size of the outstanding debt on the balance sheet, and additional borrowing will be represented as positive number, as these figures would increase the size of outstanding debt on the balance sheet. For this reason, whichever figure is selected as the smaller number we want to make sure it is correctly represented as an expense if it is a positive number and add the amount back to the debt balance if the result happens to be negative. In order to capture this, you must use a negative sign before the MIN function in your debt repayment or additional borrowing formula in cell Q42. (Example: -MIN) There are several aspects of logic that must be represented in your formula. However, the formula itself is short and fairly simple to look at. In cell Q42, debt repayment or additional borrowings, your formula should look like the following: =-MIN(Q38,Q41).

This formula will automatically decide whether the full amount of available cash flow should be used to pay down existing debt, whether only a portion of cash flow is required because there is more available cash flow than there is outstanding debt, or whether additional debt needs to be taken onto the balance sheet because cash flow was negative for the period. **It is perhaps the most important decision point in the leveraged buyout model.** Be sure to take the time to fully understand the formula and most importantly the logic behind it. Once we have completed the model, it may be worth the time to change some of the variables within the model and/or make direct changes in the debt repayment or additional borrowings line item in your leveraged buyout analysis to see the degree to which this item impacts the target company in our analysis.

It is worth noting that for virtually every prudent company there is a minimum cash amount the target company will keep on its balance sheet. As a matter of practicality, a company will almost always want to keep some cash on hand in order to make good on any short-term payables and operational costs that go hand in hand with running a business. This cash on hand is exempt from being used to pay down debts as it is essential to running the business on a short-term basis.

> It is worth noting that for virtually every prudent company there is a minimum cash amount they will keep on their balance sheet.

Before we move any further on the topic of cash, we must first decide on the amount of cash that we will assume the target company will carry in the pro forma explicit forecast range. You can look at the recent historical financials of the target company to get a better sense of what the average cash balance carried on the balance sheet of the company has been over the years. It is, generally, safe to assume that the historical balances have been satisfactory in meeting the company's short-term operating needs. For this reason, you may wish to assume that the pro forma cash balances carried on our projected balance sheet are approximately in line with historical value, while making any increase or decrease in the carried cash balance based on the projected growth or contraction of the business. We are assuming that net sales are growing at a rate of 7.0% annually, so we will assume our pro forma cash on hand is slightly larger than the cash balance of years past. We will assume that the target company will carry a cash-on-hand balance of $500 million. You may wish to make an annual adjustment to cash on hand to reflect the growth in the operations of the business. In our example, we will assume that the $500 million cash-on-hand balance is enough to cover the short-term business requirements in each year of our pro forma forecast range. That being the case, we will not need to make incremental changes to cash on hand in any of the following pro forma years.

If anyone takes objection with the assumption of a stable cash-on-hand balance, you can easily make an adjustment in the balance sheet. The real question is – Where will

> You may wish to make an annual adjustment to cash on hand to reflect the growth in the operations of the business.

the increased cash amount come from? There are primarily two sources from which the assumed increased cash on the balance sheet could come from; either positive cash flow or from borrowing the money. To make this adjustment in your pro forma financial statements, you could first denote the assumed increase in the cash-on-hand balance and then via formula direct the positive cash flow to the cash-on-hand section of the balance sheet. Once the cash balance requirement is met you can use the rest of the cash flow to pay down debt. In the event that you would prefer to use debt as the source for increasing the cash on hand, you would add the additional cash requirement to the debt balance, boost cash on hand to the new assumed required level and continue to pay down debt with any positive cash flow available to pay down debt.

We have explained the different ways in which you can handle cash on the balance sheet. In our example, we are using a stable cash on hand assumption over the pro forma explicit forecast range, as we believe this to be a sufficient amount of cash to meet the short-term business obligations of the company. It will also help in demonstrating the key points of our leveraged buyout analysis by not muddying the waters with unnecessary complication. The key aspects of cash on the balance sheet have been explained above; feel free to incorporate this logic into your leveraged buyout analysis once you have completed the example model.

Just as we did for the outstanding debt balance, we can think of one year's ending cash balance as the following year's beginning cash balance. This is important to realize because we will assume the target company will be earning interest income on the cash balances it is holding at the bank. (Presumably the target company is not storing its cash in a vault, deep in the basement at corporate headquarters and earning no interest.) Let's enter our assumed cash-on-hand balance of $500 million into the pro forma cash analysis. The $500 million should be entered as the ending cash-on-hand balance of Year 0 (P48). Just as we did for outstanding debt, let's now go ahead and make the following year's beginning cash-on-hand balance equal to the prior year's ending cash-on-hand balance. We will set Year 1 beginning cash balance equal to Year 0 ending cash balance. Your formula in cell (Q46) should look like the following: =P48.

EXCESS CASH

We have covered a number of scenarios in our model, from what happens in the event cash flow is greater than outstanding debt to what happens in the event there is negative cash flow (cash losses) available to pay down debt. One thing we have not covered is what to do in the event that cash flow available to pay down debt is greater than the actual debt that is outstanding. Where does the excess cash go?

> Where cash flow available to pay down debt is greater than the outstanding debt balance, the excess cash flow will be added to the cash-on-hand balance on the balance sheet.

In the case where cash flow available to pay down debt is greater than the outstanding debt balance, the excess cash flow will be added to the cash-on-hand balance on the balance sheet. We will not assume the target company will use this excess cash flow for any purpose other than storing it away for a rainy day. In practice, once the target company has reached the point where cash is beginning to be stockpiled on the balance sheet as cash on hand, it may be time to look at other options for using the cash towards the profitable expansion of the business.

However, that is not our concern at the moment. Right now we must first focus on implementing the correct logic to effectively locate any excess cash from cash flow available for debt paydown and the outstanding debt balance into cash on hand. Remember, from a dollar and cents perspective, the reason this is a big deal is because interest income will be calculated based on the amount of cash that is carried on our balance sheet. For that reason, we certainly want to make sure that we are taking into consideration every dollar of interest income that we have coming to us. After all, we are in business to make money.

To do this, we begin in the additions to cash on hand line item in our cash analysis. We are not concerned with Year 0 at this point, so let's start by looking at the line item in Year 1 (Q47). Here we can say that additions to cash on hand will be equal to the sum of cash flow available for debt paydown (Q38) and the paydown of outstanding debt (Q42) (which is represented as a negative number).

We have put logic in place with the debt additional borrowing or paydown (Q42) debt line item in such a way that if cash flow is negative, the additional debt borrowing line item will become a positive kick in new debt equal to the negative cash flow of the period. For that reason, we need not be concerned with ever getting a negative result for our additions to cash-on-hand line item.

Essentially, in calculating additions to cash on hand we are saying that if the target company has a positive cash flow, whatever balance of that positive cash flow is not used to pay down debt, take the remaining balance and put it in the bank as a cash deposit. Alternatively, if there is a negative cash flow for the period, we are not concerned with there being additions to cash on hand because we know from the logic we entered into the line item for additional borrowings or debt paydowns that cash on hand will not be affected. This is because any negative cash flow amount will result in a debt borrowing of an amount equal to the negative cash flow amount.

Translating this into a formula within your leveraged buyout analysis, starting in cell (Q47) your formula should look like the following: =Q38+Q42. Again, because debt paydown in cell (Q42) is represented as a negative number and additional borrowing is represented as a positive number (in the same cell), we are adding both rows together in order to determine how much cash should be added to the target company's cash on hand, should cash flow for the period exceed total outstanding debt.

With the knowledge that the logic for additions to cash on hand is functioning properly we can now complete the cash portion of our analysis by calculating the ending balance for the period. To do this, we will simply add the beginning cash-on-hand balance and the additions to cash line item to arrive at the ending cash balance. This should seem fairly intuitive.

To calculate the cash-on-hand ending balance, we focus our attention on Year 1, cell (Q48). There, add the beginning balance for cash on hand for Year 1 plus the additions for Year 1. Your formula for the ending balance for cash on hand should look like the following in cell (Q48), =sum(Q46:Q47). Doing this completes the fundamental logic and framework for the cash, debt and income portion of our analysis, which is a significant milestone in the leveraged buyout analysis process! But we still have not applied the logic across five years in our explicit forecast range. Let's do that now.

ACROSS THE FIVE YEARS

We will apply the formulas that we have carefully assembled in Year 1 of the cash flow available to pay down debt; outstanding debt; and cash on hand analyses into the remaining years of the explicit forecast period by copying the formulas from Year 1 and pasting those same formulas into the remaining years of the explicit forecast period. To do this, we start by highlighting from Year 1, net income within the cash flow available to pay down debt. Highlight down and across your spreadsheet until you reach the ending balance of cash on hand for Year 5 of the explicit forecast range. Your entire cash flow, outstanding debt, and cash-on-hand analyses for the explicit forecast range should now be highlighted. We are applying the formulas in Year 1 across the rows to Year 5, so as you may have guessed we can now complete all the remaining years of the explicit forecast range with the keyboard shortcut CTRL+R. After pressing CTRL+R, your entire forecast range for cash flow, outstanding debt, and cash on hand should be populated with estimates.

However, we are not finished with our leveraged buyout model yet! Based on the estimates for cash and debt that you were just able to construct we can now go back and determine what the estimated net interest expense will likely be for our target company.

NET INTEREST INCOME

Net interest income is a major consideration when evaluating a leveraged buyout. After all, at the end of the day we are considering how attractive is an investment to equity investors when it entails loading a target company's balance up with considerable debt. Whether or not the leveraged buyout is an attractive investment hinges a great deal on the degree to which the target company is able to service the debt expense (i.e. interest expense) and ultimately pay down outstanding debt.

A company's ability to meet regular interest expense obligations and pay down debt is determined by the firm ability to make money. Ironically, we could not compute net interest expense earlier in our income statement because you cannot determine interest expense without knowing outstanding debt and the interest rate that is being charged on the debt. Yet we cannot forecast the target company's debt balance (with the exception of Year 0) without knowing what net interest expense impact will be net income (because net income is the first component of determining cash flow available to pay down debt).

In short, the reason we skip interest income and expense in our original build of the income statement is because the net interest expense is dependent on outstanding debt, which happens to depend on the cash flow that is available to pay down debt. Essentially, each individual year's forecast for the net interest expense will rely on the prior period's earnings and the degree to which they were used to pay down debt. Each year interest expense is directly affected by what happened the previous year.

> The reason we skip interest income and expense in our original build of the income statement is because the net interest expense is dependent on outstanding debt.

We can now revisit our income statement and bring in the final pieces that make up net interest expense. We first turn our attention to the interest income portion of our calculation. As you may recall, we calculate interest income as the beginning balance of cash on hand multiplied by the paying interest rate. (Note: If you are not able to find the interest rate paid on the target company's cash-on-hand deposits explicitly identified in the annual or quarterly reports, you may also arrive at the interest rate paid by dividing interest income by cash and cash equivalents on the balance sheet.) Our example model starts from Year 0 and ending balances for Year 0 are the same as the beginning balances of Year 1. Interest begins accruing from the beginning of each year. In other words, we will be calculating interest from the beginning balance of each period. Our example does not have a period prior to Year 0, so we will calculate interest income starting in Year 1, but will assume that the cash balance at the beginning of Year 0 was the same as the ending balance.

To calculate interest income in Year 1 of the income statement multiply the beginning cash-on-hand balance of Year 1 by the interest rate paid on cash:

```
interest income = cash on hand (beginning balance) x interest
rate
```

The formula for Year 1 interest income in the income statement should look like the following: =$P$46*P48. Make sure that you anchor both the row and column identifiers of the interest rate portion of the formula as we will want to use this same component of the formula when we apply it across the different beginning cash balances of the following forecast years.

Behind these seemingly simple calculations for interest income are the more complex calculations for debt paydown and additions to cash on hand, which will have a direct impact on the amount of interest income that is earned over a period. While the face of our interest calculation is quite straightforward, there is significant calculation going on in prior calculations.

Interest expense, as we mentioned before, is a key component of the leveraged buyout analysis. We can now forecast the target company's interest expense on the income statement in a similar fashion to how we calculated interest income:

```
interest expense = outstanding debt (beginning balance) x
interest rate
```

We will again be using the beginning balance, this time for outstanding debt, and multiplying it by the appropriate interest rate, or cost of debt. For the same reasons mentioned regarding interest income, make sure you are calculating interest expense on the beginning balances of outstanding debt. With active debt paydowns in effect, we can expect that debt balances at the beginning of each year will vary significantly and that means our interest expense figures will be changing as well. Double checking that you have the correct balance referenced will save you time and embarrassment if you find you are calculating interest expense on an incorrect debt balance, not to mention it may dramatically affect the outlook of the contemplated transaction.

Let's go ahead and enter our formula for interest expense. In our example, we assume that the debt from the leveraged buyout transaction will come onto the balance sheet in the end of Year 0. Obviously, there is no paying down of debt that occurs in Year 0. Year 0 is displayed to provide a historical reference against pro forma projections and provides a starting point at which we assume the debt comes onto the balance sheet (i.e. end of Year 0). In Year 1

> Double checking that you have the correct balance referenced will save you time and embarrassment.

(F43), interest expense should be calculated as the following: =$P$41*-Q43. Notice in the example that interest expense is represented as a negative on our income statement. Since outstanding debt balance and the interest rate on debt are both positive figures, you will need to be sure to include a negative sign before one of the reference inputs. This will ensure that you are representing interest expense correctly as a reduction from earnings, rather than as a contributor to earnings.

Now that you have completed the Year 1 interest income and expense portion of the income statement there is only one item left outstanding within the income statement. Let's apply our interest income and expense formulas across the explicit forecast range to finish up the income statement. We can do this by holding down the SHIFT key and using the arrow keys to navigate and highlight the area from Year 1 interest income to Year 5 interest expense. Once the area (F43:J44) is highlighted, use the keyboard shortcut CTRL+R to apply our Year 1 formulas across the explicit forecast range. You have now completed the pro forma financial estimates for the target company in our example leveraged buyout transaction.

As you may have guessed, the scenario of annual cash flow available for debt paydown exceeding total outstanding debt will not occur during the explicit forecast range of the example leveraged buyout model that we are building. This is not the case because the amount of debt from the transaction that needs to be paid down is larger than the sum of the five years of cash flow available for debt paydown. However, you may wish to experiment with some of the model's assumptions to see how this important aspect of the model works under different scenarios. First, try adjusting the revenue growth assumptions that we assumed to be 7.0%. Rather than the approximate historical growth rate of 7.0%, let's assume that the revenue growth is that of the next hot technology start-up with estimated growth of 200% every year for the next five years. It may not be realistic, but it gets the point across. With these new revenue growth estimates we see in our cash analysis that additions to cash on hand are being recognized, as we desired. The target company will be able to both pay down its debt and begin storing away cash in no time. More precisely, before the end of Year 3 the target company will have paid down the complete amount of debt taken on during the buyout transaction and by the end of Year 5 the company will have stored away cash on hand of an estimated $234 billion. Not bad for our target company. Unfortunately for management, this is not a realistic scenario given historic performance and what we know about the company, but it proves to us that our logic for additions to cash on hand works correctly and also demonstrates the mechanics of what will take place on the target company's balance sheet once debt is paid down and additions to cash on hand commence.

STATISTICS AND RATIO ANALYSIS

The pro forma estimates for our target company are finally complete. This marks another major milestone in the creation process of our leveraged buyout model. However, we still have a few things to do before we can say that we are completely finished. Namely, some statistics must be calculated in order for the would-be investors to evaluate the potential returns of the transaction. This will be the subject of the next chapter.

In order to do this we want to make sure that we are comparing apple to apples and not apples to oranges. For that reason, let's set our Year 0 interest income and expense to that of Year 1 interest income and expense, respectively. We know that this change does not reflect historical reality, but it will allow us to compare the performance of the company under the same capital structure conditions.

That is, by making the adjustment to Year 0 interest income and expense we get the chance to compare the historic performance of the company as if it was carrying the same approximate debt on its balance sheet as assumed under the contemplated leveraged buyout transaction. (You may want to compare both the adjusted and non-adjusted capital structure returns when conducting your analysis. In our example, we will look at the historical-adjusted returns because it requires more work and the non-adjusted returns do not require anything other than comparing historically given data.)

As we mention above, let's adjust Year 0 interest income (E44) by setting it equal to Year 1 interest income. You can do this by simply entering the formula: =F44. After that, do the same thing for interest expense in Year 0 (E43) by setting it equal to Year 1 interest expense using the formula: =F43. The Year 0 income statement is now adjusted for the assumed change in capital structure. This can be done in different ways and the manner in which you choose to make the adjustment is not important. What is important is that you understand that in order to have an apples to apples comparison when it comes to financial performance, historical information should be shown on an adjusted basis (as well as a non-adjusted basis).

CHAPTER 13
RETURNS ANALYSIS

Having completed pro forma estimates is a significant accomplishment, but it still doesn't tell us how much money we can expect to make on the deal. Investors care about returns. Simply put, how much money can we expect to make off this leveraged buyout, if we put our money at risk in the deal?

A good way to measure estimated returns is by using an internal rate of return analysis or IRR analysis. IRR analysis is an effective way to measure the profitability or returns of investments. An easy way to think of IRR is as if it were the yield on a loan. When you lend a friend $100 dollars and he pays you back that $100 plus another $10 because you are such a nice person, you have realized an IRR of 10%. Another way that IRR is commonly described is the discount rate at which the net present value of all cash flows is equal to zero. We will not go into detail on that explanation, but it is good for you to know that IRR is commonly referred to as such. However, at the end of the day it is still just the $10 profit you made from risking your money. Keeping that in mind, let's move on to building our IRR analysis for the target company, based on the pro forma estimates that you just created.

> IRR analysis is an effective way to measure the profitability or returns of investments.

Just like in our example, where our friend paid us back the money we lent him, at some point in time investors are going to want to get their money back, plus a return on the investment. The only way to do that is to exit the investment by selling it to another buyer. A common practice for measuring the price paid for an investment is as a multiple of the company's earnings. Measuring purchase price as a multiple of earnings provides some context when comparing the purchase price relative to other, similar companies. Using multiples of earnings can also be used to approximate a fair purchase price as well. Say, for example, you just won the biggest poker tournament the world has ever seen and with your winnings you decide you want to buy the casino. One of the first things you are going to want to know is how much do other casinos cost to buy. If you find out that all the other casinos are valued at approximately 10.0x earnings, there better be a good reason why the casino you are attempting to buy is seeking an implied 16.0x earnings as its asking price. Using multiples of earnings levels the playing field and lets potential buyers know how much they would be spending for each dollar of earnings the company is currently and expecting to generate in the future.

In our IRR analysis we use a conservative exit multiple of 8.0x EBITDA. For the purposes of this example, let's assume that all the target company's competitors that are publicly traded trade in a range hovering around 8.0x EBITDA. Based on the fact that similar companies trade around the same multiple of earnings, we can say that 8.0x EBITDA is justifiable exit multiple. EBITDA is an ideal figure for calculate multiples because it excludes any factors concerning capital structure or financing decisions as well as tax treatments. In essence, EBITDA does a good job of leveling the field for comparison so that potential investors can get down to the business of evaluating the operations and earnings power of a company.

We begin constructing the IRR analysis by calculating the implied enterprise value of our target company by multiplying the exit multiple of 8.0x EBITDA (D69), which we explained above, by the pro forma Year 1 EBITDA figure (F49). You can think of enterprise value as the amount of money that would be required to buy the target company outright. Enterprise value is equal to the sum of common and preferred equity, debt, and minority interests less any cash on the balance sheet and the market value of ownership interests in associate companies. Your formula in cell (F70) should look like the following: =F49*$D$69. Note that we are anchoring the exit multiple of 8.0x because we will continue to use this multiple throughout our IRR analysis.

> You can think of enterprise value as the amount of money that would be required to buy the target company outright.

◇	A	B	C	D	E	F	G	H	I	J
65	IRR Analysis									
66	(Dollars in millions)									
67								Pro Forma		
68						Year 1	Year 2	Year 3	Year 4	Year 5
69	Exit EBITDA Multiple			8.0x						
70	Implied Enterprise Value					$ 16,104	$ 17,242	$ 18,461	$ 19,764	$ 21,159
71	Less: Net Debt					(10,938)	(10,505)	(10,005)	(9,432)	(8,781)
72	Implied Equity Value					$ 5,166	$ 6,738	$ 8,456	$ 10,332	$ 12,378
73										
74	Implied IRR					14.8%	22.4%	23.4%	23.1%	22.4%
75	Implied Multiple of Capital					1.1x	1.5x	1.9x	2.3x	2.8x

IRR analysis

In order to calculate the implied equity value of the target company, which is what we as equity investors are most concerned with, we must subtract the net debt from the implied enterprise value we just calculated. Net debt is simply the company's outstanding short-term and long-term debt less cash and cash equivalents on the balance sheet:

```
net debt = short-term debt + long-term debt - cash and cash
equivalents
```

In our IRR analysis, still in Year 1, we will calculate net debt by setting our formula equal to the outstanding debt balance of Year 1 (Q43) less the cash on hand ending balance of Year 1 (Q48). In our example analysis we are representing the net debt as a negative number because we are subtracting it from the implied enterprise value. For that reason, we need to place a negative sign at the beginning of the net debt formula. Your formula for Year 1 net debt in cell Q8 should look like the following: =-(Q43-Q48)

From here we can calculate the implied equity value, which is simply the result of subtracting net debt from implied enterprise value:

```
implied equity value = implied enterprise value - net debt
```

Since we have already taken the step to represent net debt as a negative number, all we need to do is sum the two figures to arrive at the target company's implied equity value in Year 1. Your formula in cell (F72) should look like the following: =sum(F70:F71). Try using the keyboard shortcut ALT+EQUALS to calculate the formula in as few key strokes as possible. We can see that from the prospective initial equity investment of $4,500, our projections show that implied equity value has already grown to $5,166 by the end of Year 1. In other words, we expect equity value to have increased by over $660 million. But is just comparing the absolute implied equity value the only way to go about measuring performance?

The short answer is, No. We can use the internal rate of return to measure returns performance on a relative basis, which when combined with absolute returns figures, can give prospective investors a much fuller picture on a potential investment. When it comes to measuring performance, generally speaking, more is more. The more angles from which you can assess an investment, the more comprehensive your analysis and that makes potential investors more comfortable.

Looking at the first year's implied equity value, we want to calculate the internal rate of return for Year 1 in order to get an understanding of the target company's pro forma performance on a relative basis. We want to know what kind of returns on the investors' money, in percentage terms, we are forecasting with the given assumptions of the model. In order to do this, we will need to calculate the rate of return, which is a function of the amount of money put into the investment, the amount of money investors expect to get out of the investment (including periodic dividends and the lump sum upon selling the investment), and the amount of time taken to realize returns. In our example, we do not expect the target company to be paying out dividends over the explicit forecast range. Instead, the company will be focused on using earnings to pay down debt.

We can calculate the expected IRR by using the RATE function in our spreadsheet. In Year 1 (F74), we will use the following formula: =RATE(F68,0,-$F$12,F72). Let's translate this formula into common language. The RATE formula is broken down into a few pieces. The first is the number of periods, which is understood to be years. We are in Year 1, so there is only one period so far and we are referencing cell (F68) because this cell has a numerical value of one. The second component of the RATE function is payment. As we mentioned, there are no paid dividends estimated for the target company in the forecasted periods, so the incremental payments are zero. (If we were calculating a rate of interest for a loan, we would enter the interest payments in this section and that would be used to determine the cost of the loan.) The next component of the

RATE function is present value (of investment). This amount is entered as a negative number because the cash is leaving the bank account of the investor and going towards the purchase of the investment. (Note that this figure is anchored because we will be using the same number in all of the following years' IRR calculations.) The final consideration in our rate of return formula is future value (of investment). This is the estimated pro forma dollar amount that an investor would sell the investment for and have the funds placed into their bank account. This figure is of course a positive number because it is money that will be received at the point of sale. These four components come together to calculate the forecasted internal rate of return for the target company in the pro forma Year 1. When computed, we see that the internal rate of return is projected to be approximately 14.8% if the company were sold one year after the initial investment.

MULTIPLE OF MONEY

Another metric often used to measure returns is the multiple of money:

```
multiple of money = implied equity value / equity investment
```

This metric is quick and easy to understand because it provides a relative measure of how much money was returned on an investment to how much money was actually invested. The major shortcoming of this statistic is that it does not take into consideration the time it takes to realize returns on investment. What good is a return of 2,000% to you as a business owner if it takes 200 years to realize that return? You will already be dead! Your great grandchildren may be appreciative though.

> 'Multiple of money' provides a relative measure of how much money was returned on an investment to how much money was actually invested.

Let's go ahead and calculate the implied multiple of money in the returns analysis portion of our model, directly below implied IRR, which we just calculated. We begin by setting Year 1 (F75) equal to the implied equity value of pro forma Year 1 and then divide by the initial equity investment, which we originally assumed at the beginning of our model to be $4,500 million. In formula form, your equation should look like the following: =F72/$F$12. We will anchor the initial equity investment reference in our formula because it will be used in subsequent formulas to calculate multiple of money in the following pro forma years. Once you have the formula in place, you should have a resulting multiple of money figure of 1.1x.

RETURNS IN THE FUTURE

Now that we have calculated implied equity value along with implied internal rate of return and the implied multiple of money for pro forma Year 1 we can apply the same formulas across the remaining pro forma years to determine what the implied returns are in the later years of the investment.

We can do this in a few keys strokes using the CTRL+R keyboard shortcut. First, highlight the area from pro forma Year 1 implied enterprise value down and across to pro forma Year 5 implied multiple of money. Once we have the desired area highlighted press CTRL+R. Your formulas should be applied across the pro forma years all the way to Year 5. All of our anchoring was put in place for the formulas created in the Year 1 calculations and for that reason we are able to apply the same formulas across the future years.

If we look at the results of our forecast, we see that implied equity value continues to build over the explicit forecast range, which should not be too surprising to us at this point. And naturally, the implied multiple of money also continues to increase over the pro forma years as equity values increase. What is a little more interesting, however, is that the implied IRR peaks in Year 3. Why is that?

As we mentioned, the multiple of money calculation does not take into consideration time or the time value of money. So, of course, as long as equity value increases the multiple of money statistic will continue to increase. (This is a positive thing!) However, IRR does take into consideration the timing of returns. For that reason, we see that the implied internal rate of return peaks in Year 3. It would take accelerated revenue growth or increased cost reduction (or both) to see increasing IRR after Year 3. For reasons like this, professional investors do not only rely on one metric to provide them with insight on the attractiveness of an investment. Investors will have to look at the calculations such as these and make a determination as to when it would be ideal to exit an investment. The decision will most likely be based on a number of considerations. The first will be whether or not a buyer can be located. After all, every transaction needs a buyer and a seller, but other considerations will include what other opportunities exist in the market and whether the potential returns from another investment outperform the returns of the current investment. This is a simplified view of an investor, as

> The bottom line for every investor is – Where can I get the most for my money? These ratios help them measure that.

there are countless considerations that must be accounted for. However, the bottom line for every investor is – Where can I get the most for my money? These two ratios help an investor measure what they will get for their money in this investment from different angles.

CHAPTER 14

ADDITIONAL RATIO ANALYSIS

Ratios are a means of measuring a given company's performance over different periods of time. Some ratios that are very common in leveraged buyout analysis include:

- total debt to equity

- total debt to capital

- total debt to EBITDA

- net debt to EBITDA

- EBITDA to interest

- EBIT to interest.

We will discuss each of these ratios and explain how to calculate them in our example model.

Before we dive into the calculations of our ratios we must first forecast any changes to shareholders' equity. Let's turn our attention to the shareholders' analysis portion of our spreadsheet. We will calculate changes in shareholders' equity by first establishing what our equity value would be in Year 0, at the point just after completion of the leveraged buyout transaction. Year 0 shareholders' equity will be equal to the initial equity investment minus the transaction fees. Your formula in cell (P54) should look like the following: =F12-F8. (We are assuming purchase accounting.)

The beginning shareholders' equity balance in Year 1 will be equal to the ending balance in Year 0. Therefore, you will want to set your Year 1 beginning balance in cell (Q52) equal to the formula: =P54. This should be straightforward. In order to arrive at the ending balance for shareholders' equity we would need to normally add net income after subtracting out any dividends and also take into consideration any stock repurchases or issuances made by the company. In our example, the company is not issuing nor is it purchasing back any of its stock. We assume that the company will not being paying a dividend over the explicit forecast range. For this reason, we can arrive at changes to shareholders' equity/retained earnings by just referencing pro forma net income for the period. Your formula for changes to shareholders' equity in Year 1 (Q53) should look like the following: =F47

◇	L	M	N	O	P	Q	R	S	T	U
50	ABC Company									
51	**Shareholders' Equity**									
52	Beginning Balance					$ 4,400	$ 5,093	$ 5,870	$ 6,737	$ 7,703
53	Plus: Net Income					693	777	868	966	1,072
54	Ending Balance				$ 4,400	$ 5,093	$ 5,870	$ 6,737	$ 7,703	$ 8,775

Shareholders' equity

All of our assumptions are reasonable, as long as we believe the new owners of the company will carry this strategy out in practice. If you are unsure, you can model alternative scenarios to forecast out the performance of the target company under alternative circumstances. It is more likely than not that you will want to look at several different scenarios in building your analysis.

As you may have guessed, in order to arrive at the ending balance for shareholders' equity we simply need to add our beginning balance with changes to shareholders' equity/retained earnings. Your formula for shareholders' equity ending balance should look like the following: =SUM(Q52:Q53)

Use the keyboard shortcut ALT+EQUALS to calculate shareholders' equity ending balance and save yourself a few key strokes at the same time.

Now that you have completed forecasting the changes in shareholders' equity for Year 1, let's complete the forecasts for all of the following pro forma years. In order to do this, begin by going to the beginning balance of shareholders' equity for Year 1. Hold down the SHIFT key and use the arrow keys to navigate down and across to the ending balance of shareholders' equity in Year 5 to highlight the entire pro forma area of the shareholders' equity analysis. We can use our CTRL+R shortcut to apply the same logic that we created for Year 1 across the remaining pro forma years. You have now completed the pro forma shareholders' equity analysis.

Our final concern at this point is measuring the leverage and credit statistics of our target company. For this we will take a look at each statistic. We want to understand both how to calculate the statistics and what they are telling us.

DEBT RATIOS

TOTAL DEBT TO EQUITY

Total debt to equity measures the leverage that our company is using to finance the assets on its balance sheet. A low debt to equity ratio is considered a conservative approach to financing the assets on a company's balance sheet. A higher debt to equity ratio on the other hand is considered more aggressive, as there will be additional interest expense which will increase the risk of default if revenues decline over time. In our example model, we are analyzing the target company under the assumption that it is financing the assets on its balance sheet with much more debt. This is considered considerably riskier than its current capital structure, which consists of very little debt financing and subsequently incurs very little interest expense.

In order to calculate the total debt to equity ratio in the credit and leverage statistics section of our analysis we will use the ending balances from our outstanding debt analysis as well as from our shareholders' equity analysis. Starting in Year 0, we divide Year 0 outstanding debt ending balance by Year 0 shareholders' equity ending balance. Your formula in cell (P63) should look like the following: =P43/P54

	L	M	N	O	P	Q	R	S	T	U
56	**Ratios Analysis**									
57	Total Debt / EBITDA				6.3x	5.7x	5.1x	4.6x	4.0x	3.5x
58	Net Debt / EBITDA				6.0x	5.4x	4.9x	4.3x	3.8x	3.3x
59										
60	EBITDA / Interest				3.5x	3.8x	4.2x	4.7x	5.2x	5.9x
61	EBIT / Interest				2.8x	3.0x	3.3x	3.7x	4.1x	4.7x
62										
63	Total Debt / Equity				2.7x	2.2x	1.9x	1.6x	1.3x	1.1x
64	Total Debt / Capital				72.9%	69.2%	65.2%	60.9%	56.3%	51.4%

Ratios analysis

TOTAL DEBT TO CAPITAL

Total debt to capital is similar to total debt to equity only it is not displayed as a ratio, but rather as a percentage. Total debt to capital shows debt as a percentage of both debt and equity held on our target company's balance sheet. It also shows the degree to which our target company would be financing its balance sheet with debt. By looking at this statistic we can quickly see the relative degree of leverage our target company would be using under the assumed capital structure. Like total debt to equity, it is an effective statistic for comparing the leverage of a company over time to monitor whether a company is levering up or down its balance sheet.

In order to calculate total debt to capital (Year 0), we will divide the outstanding debt ending balance by the sum of Year 0 outstanding debt ending balance and shareholders' equity ending balance. Your formula in cell (P64) should look like following: =P43/(P43+P54); in other words:

```
total debt to capital = outstanding debt (end of year) /
[outstanding debt (end of year) + shareholders' equity (end
of year)]
```

TOTAL DEBT TO EBITDA

Total debt to EBITDA is the next metric we will calculate for the target company. Credit rating agencies often use this statistic to measure the ability of a company to service its debt. A higher debt to EBITDA ratio signals a higher chance of default. This could provide rating agencies reason to lower the credit rating of a company. Total Debt to EBITDA provides a measurement of a company's ability to pay down its debt and also indicates the approximate amount of time it would take a company to pay down its debt using earnings before interest and tax expense and ignoring non-cash expenses such as depreciation and amortization.

We will calculate total debt to EBITDA for Year 0 by dividing the outstanding debt ending balance (Year 0) by the Year 0 EBITDA figure. Your formula in cell (P57) should look like the following: =P43/E49

Another metric, very similar to our last ratio, is the net debt to EBITDA ratio. We will use this statistic in our ratios analysis to measure how well the target company is positioned to pay down its debt by taking into consideration both its cash on the balance sheet as well as the company's EBITDA. Credit rating agencies also look at net debt to EBITDA to measure a company's leverage and risk of default. High ratios indicate a higher risk of default.

We calculate net debt to EBITDA in our analysis for Year 0 by first subtracting cash-on-hand ending balance (Year 0) from the outstanding debt balance at the end of Year 0. That figure is then divided by the EBITDA figure for Year 0. Your formula for net debt to EBITDA (P58) should look like the following: =(P43-P48)/E49; in other words:

```
net debt to EBITDA = (total outstanding debt - cash on hand)
/ EBITDA
```

COVERAGE RATIOS

As part of our leveraged buyout analysis, we want to be certain that the target company can generate enough earnings to at least meet the interest expense that comes along with the new leverage placed on its balance sheet. The **EBITDA to interest coverage ratio** is a means of drawing some conclusions about the ability to meet interest payments with the company's EBITDA. An EBITDA to interest expense ratio of at least 1.0x indicates that the company's EBITDA is large enough to pay off its interest expense obligation. However, this figure does not take into consideration any capital expenditures the company makes, so it is completely within the realm of possibility that a company could have a EBITDA to interest expense ratio greater than 1.0x and not be able to meet its interest expense for a period because money was used towards a capital expenditure.

> We want to be certain that the target company can generate enough earnings to at least meet the interest expense that comes along with the new leverage on its balance sheet.

Let's calculate the EBITDA to interest coverage ratio. In Year 0 of our ratios analysis, in order to calculate the EBITDA to interest coverage ratio, we want to divide the Year 0 EBITDA figure by interest expense for Year 0. Note that interest expense is represented as a negative number in our analysis, so in order for this ratio to be represented correctly you will need to have a negative sign in front of one of the inputs in your formula. Your formula for the EBITDA to interest coverage ratio (P60) in Year 0 should look like the following: =E49/-E43

You may wish to keep it in front of interest expense if it helps to keep your thoughts organized, but either way the result will be the same. If you were to omit the negative sign in the formula your result would indicate that EBITDA was negative … and that could cause some issues with the credit ratings agencies!

The final statistic that we will calculate in the ratio analysis portion of our leveraged buyout analysis is the **EBIT to interest coverage ratio**. This coverage ratio is similar to the previous EBITDA to interest coverage ratio, as it is intended to measure the company's ability to pay interest expense in a given period. The main difference is that this interest coverage ratio recognizes the accounting costs of depreciation and amortization, whereas the EBITDA coverage ratio is more concerned with measuring ability to pay interest expense from a cash perspective. Both of these interest coverage ratios provide a slightly different insight on the company's earnings power relative to the cost of debt financing.

In order to calculate the EBIT to interest coverage ratio in Year 0 we will need to divide earnings before interest and tax expense, in this case operating income, of Year 0 by the interest expense of Year 0. Again, we will need to use a negative sign before one of the two inputs in our spreadsheet because interest expense is represented as a negative number in our analysis. Your formula for EBIT to interest coverage should look like the following: =E42/-E43

Both the EBITDA and EBIT interest coverage ratios provide a view into a company's ability to meet its interest expense obligations. Higher coverage ratios imply a lower risk of default, as earnings are greater than the interest expense owed by the company. While these two coverage ratios are intended to measure the target company's ability to pay interest expense, they measure it in slightly different ways that help to give a fuller understanding of the target company's financial situation. Perhaps most importantly, the two ratios differentiate between the ability to pay in real cash terms and non-cash terms.

*　　*　　*

Ratio analysis helps us to get a more complete understanding of the target company's financial situation and also identify trends that may not be as readily apparent by simply looking at the financials of a company over a given period of time. We have calculated total debt to equity, total debt to capital, total debt to EBITDA, net debt to EBITDA, as well as coverage ratios EBITDA and EBIT to interest expense – all for Year 0. Let's use our same calculations and apply them across the explicit forecast range to measure how our credit and leverage statistics will change in relation to our financial forecast for the target company. We do this by highlighting the desired ratio analysis area from Year 0 total debt to equity to Year 5 EBIT to interest coverage. The areas from cell (P39:U46) should now be covered. Let's apply our ratios across the pro forma forecast period by using the keyboard shortcut CTRL+R. That should fill in the entire ratio analysis portion of our leverage buyout model.

Looking at the results of the ratios analysis, we see that leverage ratios indicate that the debt to equity and debt to capital ratios look to improve over the five-year period. The leverage

> Ratio analysis provides a deeper understanding and measurement of the financial health of the target company.

ratios demonstrate the company is able to lower the amount of debt on its balance sheet relative to equity over the next five years. Similarly, total and net debt to EBITDA ratios also show the size of the target company's debt steadily shrinking relative to EBITDA in each year. Finally, both coverage ratios indicate that as each year passes the target company will strengthen its ability to pay interest owed. There are no glaring inconsistencies among our ratios and the trend in decreased leverage is consistent with the rest of our analysis. Overall, our ratio analysis provides a deeper understanding and measurement of the financial health of the target company and also helps to more easily identify financial trends about the company.

CHAPTER 15

SENSITIVITY ANALYSIS

Sensitivity analyses are generally created to evaluate the degree to which outcomes would change if an input were changed. This sort of analysis is very common in discounted cash flow analysis whereby a sensitivity analysis is created to measure how much the valuation of a company changes given different discount rates or changing exit EBITDA multiples. The ability to create insightful sensitivity analyses is a valuable skill in financial analysis and modeling. Let's build our own sensitivity analysis for the target company now. We will want to see how returns (IRR) are affected with changes in the amount of equity that is invested in the transaction as well as how exit EBITDA multiples affect returns.

We start by recognizing that in the final year of our pro forma analysis we estimate an implied IRR of 22.4%. This assumes an initial equity investment of $4,500 million and an exit EBITDA multiple of 8.0x. We will use these numbers for the base case of our analysis and build from here.

> Being able to create insightful sensitivity analyses is a valuable skill in financial analysis and modeling.

We reference the base case implied IRR of 22.4% in the top lefthand corner by using the formula, =J74. It is critical that your reference is correct. A simple number entry will not work as we build out the sensitivity analysis; the calculations rely on formulas and cannot work with simple number entry. Looking at the framework of our sensitivity analysis, our row input variable is initial equity investment and the column input variable is exit EBITDA multiple. You want to make sure that your row and column inputs are a wide enough range to provide some meaningful insight regarding how returns are affected by changes in the variables. However, the input range should also be realistic. A variable range that is too wide doesn't accomplish the goal of providing meaningful comparison. For example, if you wanted to see a sensitivity analysis for returns based on the amount of money you invested in a company, you probably have some idea of approximately how much money you are looking to invest. In fact, you may have a maximum amount of money you would be willing to invest as well as a minimum amount you would need to invest in order for the investment to be worth your time. For that reason, it would not make sense to create a sensitivity analysis that starts with an investment of $1 and ranges far beyond your maximum investment amount. Instead, you would most likely prefer to see a base case figure – a number that you believe you want to invest. Then from there you would create a reasonable range around that number. From this type of information you would be in a better situation to make a decision regarding your potential investment.

In our example, the base case equity investment is $4,500 million and the base case exit EBITDA multiple is 8.0x. In our sensitivity analysis we will use an investment range of $3,500 to $5,500 million and an exit EBITDA multiple of 6.0x to 10.0x.

◇	L	M	N	O	P	Q	R
66	5 Year IRR- Sensitivity Analysis						
67					New Equity Injection		
68		22.4%	$ 3,500	$ 4,000	$ 4,500	$ 5,000	$ 5,500
69	Exit	6.0x	11.1%	10.2%	9.5%	8.9%	8.4%
70	EBITDA	7.0x	19.6%	18.0%	16.7%	15.6%	14.6%
71	Multiple	8.0x	26.2%	24.2%	22.4%	21.0%	19.7%
72		9.0x	31.7%	29.3%	27.3%	25.6%	24.1%
73		10.0x	36.4%	33.7%	31.5%	29.5%	27.9%

Sensitivity analysis

Now that we have our sensitivity framework set-up, let's complete the analysis. We begin by highlighting the area from our referenced implied IRR figure (M68) down and across to cross cell between $5,500 million and 10.0x (R73). Once the area is highlighted, we want to use what is called a *data table* to create the analysis for us. In order to create a data table, press ALT+D, and then T. This is another useful keyboard shortcut that makes short work of using Data Tables. A data table pop-up screen will ask for row and column inputs. For row inputs, reference our base case equity investment figure from the model, cell ($F$12), and double check that the reference is hard anchored for both the column and row figure. After inputting the row reference cell, input the column reference cell as the exit EBITDA multiple, cell (`$D$69`). This figure should also be hard anchored for both row and column. Press ENTER and the data table should populate with a complete sensitivity analysis.

We can see from the sensitivity analysis that the implied rate of return is greater with relatively smaller amounts of equity investment (i.e. more leverage) and larger exit multiples. This should not come as a surprise. The value of the sensitivity analysis is that it provides a much better idea of the degree to which the implied IRR changes with different variables. The sensitivity of returns will almost always be of interest to investors when assessing an investment opportunity. The analysis is an excellent way to present a range of outcomes that can occur under different circumstances. This gives potential investors a greater level of comfort in understanding investment opportunities and can be one of the ultimate points of consideration for an investment opportunity.

> The sensitivity of returns will almost always be of interest to investors when assessing an investment opportunity.

CONCLUSION

Creating a thorough leveraged buyout analysis requires the financial analyst to carefully examine several factors and scenarios regarding the target company and the leverage to be used in its purchase. As a practitioner in the corporate finance industry it is important to create an analysis that is accurate in reflecting, as best as possible, the current condition of the target company – and also flexible in considering the potential for different scenarios in the target company's future operating environment or performance. It is important to establish a clear picture of the current financial condition of the company and then lay out the different outcomes that could arise based on the company's future performance. This includes the company's ability to profitably grow the business and ultimately generate returns for the owners and investors in the company. By understanding the fundamental techniques and principles underlying LBO analysis and by working through the model in this book, you should be able to develop a deeper understanding of the investor's perspective and ultimately be able to use these techniques as a practitioner in the financial industry whether it be in investment banking or private equity or some other field.

> It is important to create an analysis that reflects, as best as possible, the current condition of the target company – and is also flexible in considering the potential for different scenarios.

Finally, as you work through building the example LBO model analysis, or any other analysis, be certain to explore using different variables and assumptions to see how any changes will affect the forecasted performance of the target company. This will not only help in your understanding of the target company and the contemplated transaction, but more importantly it will help to reinforce some of the fundamental principles that are behind every leveraged buyout transaction. As always, the most important factor to understanding and development is repetition. For the MS Excel version of the example model used in this book – complete with a template, formulas, and completed version of the LBO analysis – go to **www.fin-models.com**.

> As always, the most important factor to understanding and development is repetition.

INDEX

OPTIMISING DISTRESSED LOAN BOOKS

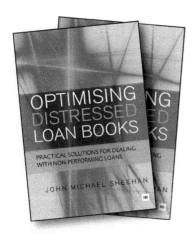

PRACTICAL SOLUTIONS FOR DEALING WITH NON-PERFORMING LOANS

by John Michael Sheehan

I N THIS UNIQUE NEW BOOK, John Michael Sheehan explains why financial institutions have failed to resolve distressed loan books profitably in the past and describes the solutions they can put in place to improve this in the future. Sheehan builds on 20 years' experience of hands-on asset monetisation, loan portfolio servicing and debt work-out to describe how banks can learn to convert the dredges of loan defaults into profits. Written in a clear and approachable style, illustrated throughout and punctuated with insightful real-life case studies, Sheehan provides a highly accessible guide to this technical area.

The book is divided into three parts. The first section analyses how and why banks fail to maximise distressed recoveries. The second section is a practical, basic training manual of techniques, systems and processes that will explain to investors or lenders how to go about earning back their losses and, in many cases, clearing amounts greater than par. The final section analyses lessons from previous crises and proposes how in the future financial institutions can improve their distressed loan resolution practices.

Bank executives and officers, their advisors, loan servicers, investors, and government-sponsored entities will be able to use this book as a working tool to assist them in working-out loans and retaining the rewards from this process. Accountants, administrators and ratings agencies should find this book to be an extremely useful source of reference, whilst regulators, academics and students will also find it will improve their understanding of the secretive distressed debt industry and therefore the financial system.

www.harriman-house.com/optimisingdistressedloanbooks

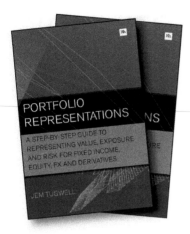

PORTFOLIO
REPRESENTATIONS

A STEP-BY-STEP GUIDE TO REPRESENTING VALUE, EXPOSURE AND RISK FOR FIXED INCOME, EQUITY, FX AND DERIVATIVES

by Jem Tugwell

THIS BOOK PROVIDES A PRACTICAL and sophisticated insight into each financial asset type, and how the different risks and exposures they involve should be most accurately combined and represented in a portfolio.

The financial issues facing the world since the late 2000s have provided the asset management community with a brutal reminder of the importance of having genuine knowledge of portfolio structures and the risks embedded within them. More so than ever, fund managers need a clear and consistent way of separating value from exposure in their portfolios, allowing a complete 'look-through' to the real risks contained in derivatives and pooled/structured products.

Equally, as fund managers are driven to find risk-adjusted rather than just raw returns, it is imperative that risk measures and the understanding derived from them are applied to the entirety of a portfolio, as opposed to just particular asset classes or sections.

This book, written by hugely experienced investment expert Jem Tugwell, provides a practical and comprehensive solution. Written in plain English and carefully structured to be easy to use, this is the definitive guide to accurately and quickly representing value in financial portfolios of every complexity.

www.harriman-house.com/portfoliorepresentations

THE OPERATIONAL RISK
HANDBOOK
FOR FINANCIAL COMPANIES

A GUIDE TO THE NEW WORLD OF
PERFORMANCE-ORIENTED
OPERATIONAL RISK

by Brian Barnier

T HE OPERATIONAL RISK HANDBOOK for Financial Companies is a groundbreaking new book. It seeks to apply for the first time a range of proven operational risk techniques from other industries and disciplines to the troubled territory of financial services.

Operational risk expert Brian Barnier introduces a range of sophisticated, dependable and – crucially – approachable tools for risk evaluation, risk response and risk governance. He provides a more robust way of gaining a better picture of risks, shows how to build risk-return awareness into decision making, and how to fix (and not just report) risks.

The practical importance of fully understanding and acting on risk to the business begins in the foreword on plan-B thinking, penned by Marshall Carter, chairman of the NYSE and deputy chairman of NYSE Euronext.

Suitable for companies of all sizes, this book is of direct relevance and use to all business managers, practitioners, boards and senior executives. Key insights from and for each are built into every chapter, including unique contributions from board members of a range of companies.

The Operational Risk Handbook for Financial Companies is an essential book for making better decisions at every level of a financial company; ones that measurably improve outcomes for boards, managers, employees and shareholders alike.

www.harriman-house.com/operationalriskhandbookforfinancialcompanies

THE ULTRA HIGH NET WORTH
BANKER'S HANDBOOK

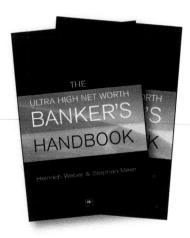

by Heinrich Weber
and Stephen Meier

T HIS BOOK IS FOR PRIVATE BANKERS who work or aim to work in the Ultra High Net Worth field, the most sought-after and secluded high-end client segment of private banking and wealth management. For UHNW clients, this book is a guide on how to deal with your bankers and what you can expect from them, depicting the view from the other side of the table. And for the management of a private bank or private banking division of a financial institution, this book will serve as an essential introduction on how to improve performance.

Expert, in-depth and accessible, *The Ultra High Net Worth Banker's Handbook* is the ultimate guide to this area of modern finance.

Estimates show that there are around 20,000 Ultra High Net Worth individuals in existence today, each with bankable assets in excess of $50 million. Between them they possess a wealth of $5,000 billion, 10% of the world's estimated total wealth. The UHNW wealth management business is therefore a critically important as well as complex part of modern finance. It exists within a "client-banker-bank" triangle and is influenced by serious exogenous factors in political, economic and fiscal environments, as well as by numerous emotional, familial and personal dimensions. In this book the authors address these complex relationships, serving as guides and advisors for UHNW bankers, banks and clients alike.

www.harriman-house.com/ultrahighnetworthbankershbook